Peninsular War and Waterloo 1808–15

British Rifleman

VERSUS

French Skirmisher

COMBAT

David Greentree

Illustrated by Adam Hook

OSPREY PUBLISHING
Bloomsbury Publishing Plc

Kemp House, Chawley Park, Cumnor Hill, Oxford OX2 9PH, UK
29 Earlsfort Terrace, Dublin 2, Ireland
1385 Broadway, 5th Floor, New York, NY 10018, USA
Email: info@ospreypublishing.com

OSPREY is a trademark of Osprey Publishing Ltd

First published in Great Britain in 2020

Print ISBN: 978 1 4728 3184 2
ePub: 978 1 4728 3209 2
ePDF: 978 1 4728 3208 5
XML: 978 1 4728 3207 8

Maps by www.bounford.com
Index by Rob Munro
Typeset by PDQ Digital Media Solutions, Bungay, UK
Printed and bound in India by Replika Press Private Ltd.

www.ospreypublishing.com
To find out more about our authors and books visit our website. Here
you will find extracts, author interviews, details of forthcoming events
and the option to sign-up for our newsletter.

Acknowledgements

I would like to thank the series editor, Nick Reynolds, for assisting with
the search for images for the book, and David Campbell who provided
many useful sources and suggestions.

Editor's note

During the early 19th century, British infantry regiments were usually
numbered, and referred to as regiments of 'Foot' to distinguish them
from regiments of 'Horse' (i.e. cavalry). In this book, the shortened form
(e.g. '29th Foot') is used. While some regiments fielded more than one
battalion, others did not; in this book, the battalion number is given
(e.g. '1/31st Foot') where appropriate, while regiments that fielded only
one battalion are given simply as '29th Foot'. As the 95th Regiment
of Foot (Rifles) is featured prominently in this book, the term '95th' is
used to refer to the whole of the regiment, while '2/95th' refers to the
2nd Battalion of the regiment. Similarly, the 60th (Royal American)
Regiment of Foot is referred to simply as the '60th', with individual
battalions of that regiment being referred to in the form '5/60th'.

The Napoleonic-era French line-infantry regiment was designated
régiment d'infanterie de ligne, here given in the shortened form as 'Ligne'.
French light-infantry regiments were usually given the title *régiment
d'infanterie légère*, here given in the shortened form as 'Léger'. Both types
of regiment usually had more than one battalion; in this book, individual
battalions are referred to in the shortened form, so the 2nd Battalion of
the 32nd Light Infantry Regiment is given as '2/32ᵉ Léger'.

Many of the images in this book come from the superb holdings of the
Anne S.K. Brown Military Collection, Brown University Library, based
at Providence, Rhode Island, USA. These illustrations are credited to
'ASKB'.

Artist's note

Readers may care to note that the original paintings from which the
colour plates in this book were prepared are available for private sale.
All reproduction copyright whatsoever is retained by the publishers. All
enquiries should be addressed to:

Scorpio, 158 Mill Road, Hailsham, East Sussex BN27 2SH, UK
Email: scorpiopaintings@btinternet.com

The publishers regret that they can enter into no correspondence upon
this matter.

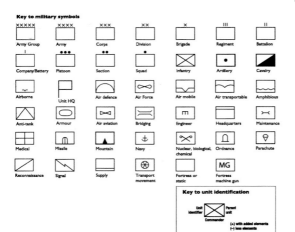

CONTENTS

Introduction

By the early evening of 18 June 1815, Major Georg Baring was in a desperate situation. His men of the 2nd Light Battalion of the King's German Legion (KGL) were responsible for holding the farm of La Haye Sainte in the centre of the Duke of Wellington's position at Waterloo and had resolutely held the French at bay since the start of the day, repelling attacks on the main gate and on the barricaded barn entrance. Utilizing the rifle rather than the musket, Baring's soldiers had caused severe casualties to the enemy; supplies of rifle balls and cartridges were limited, however, and musket balls could not be used instead as they were bigger. The French had no such problems and with defensive fire wilting gained the loopholes in the courtyard wall and began to use axes to bring down the main gate. Baring was close to ordering a retreat that would put Wellington's entire position at risk.

The flintlock musket the French were using had dominated 18th-century warfare. Training revolved around enabling the soldier to load and fire rapidly in the heat of battle and some were even told to close their eyes after pulling the trigger to protect themselves against the gunpowder's discharge. With an effective range of only 100yd, the musket was pointed in the general direction of the enemy and not aimed. Only a very small percentage of soldiers either killed with their musket or were killed by those of their enemy. This explains why soldiers were formed in long, closely packed lines to permit massed fire towards the enemy that was more likely to hit and psychologically unbalance him.

The rifle was used in a completely different way. In 18th-century North America, German colonists had introduced what were known as Pennsylvanian long rifles; characterized by a long barrel and a small bore, these weapons were used by trappers to fire a small bullet that did not make a hole in the animal's pelt when hitting the target. The grooves of the rifled barrel made the bullet spin to ensure accurate flight and increased the range. The round needed to have a tight fit in the barrel to ensure the

grooves imparted the required spin and the weapon took longer to load; however, the bullet would go where the weapon was pointed, unlike that of the musket, and could hit the target with the first shot. There were very few rifles in Britain, however, and so in 1798 the Board of Ordnance purchased 5,000 Prussian rifles at 33s each (a musket cost 15s). Riflemen were not deployed in long, close-order lines; instead, they dispersed to find cover and selected individual targets.

Operational movement on the 18th-century battlefield tended to stress advancing in line towards the enemy in order to permit a devastating fire. There was some consideration given to movement in column formation in order to speed up the approach to the enemy, but deployment into line was the central plank of tactical thinking. In France, some thought was given to the use of light troops to carry out aimed fire, but this predominantly centred on siege warfare though some advocated their use on the battlefield. In the 1790s the British Army's Lieutenant-General Sir David Dundas was in favour of the Prussian mode of warfare that induced the enemy to flee by threatening to close with the bayonet after giving fire at close range. The enemy line could be softened up with fire from artillery and skirmishers; because the light troops were dispersed and offered less of a target, they could operate close to the enemy line. Even so, rifles were not part of Dundas's doctrine, as the weapons were expensive and training needed to include complicated evolutions to load and fire; this is why the Board of Ordnance had no rifles in 1793. Light infantry, Dundas thought, should only have muskets. Rifles were costly to manufacture, difficult to maintain as the grooves clogged up with gunpowder, and slow to load.

Operationally, though, the use of light troops – especially those armed with rifles – in difficult terrain during the American Revolutionary War (1775–83) had given a decisive advantage when compared to line regiments, which operated in rigid formations and were prone to becoming disordered in broken terrain. At first, light-infantry battalions were only temporary creations, but by the time of the Napoleonic Wars (1803–15) the British

Rifles were not universally accepted by senior British Army generals as they had a slow rate of fire; they offered longer range (400yd) than the musket, however, and the grooves of the rifled barrel imparted a spin to the rifle ball that greatly improved accuracy. Riflemen practised marksmanship and trained to hit moving targets. The rifle, shorter than the musket, could be loaded while lying on the ground. To take advantage of cover, riflemen were trained to skirmish in open order and had to be relied upon to use their own initiative; their officers and NCOs, often rifle-armed themselves, were also given more latitude to take advantage of the situation and use their own initiative. Rifle training emphasized giving recruits more freedom to find suitable firing positions and targets. Here, a re-enactor dressed as a rifleman of the 95th fires his weapon from a kneeling position. (Peter John Dickson/ Getty Images)

and French armies had permanent light-infantry regimental establishments and every line battalion also had a light company, made up of personnel termed *voltigeurs* ('vaulters') in the French Army. They were given this name because when cavalry were detailed to transport them to the places where their presence was needed, the *voltigeurs* would climb on the horse and ride pillion and then descend to form up rapidly and follow on at the trot. Throughout the French Revolutionary Wars (1792–1802) and the Napoleonic Wars, light infantry of both sides covered the advance of attack columns and fought in built-up terrain where special composite battalions could be formed, especially during sieges. If a certain terrain feature had to be captured, elite companies (light infantry and grenadiers) could be brought together to complete a task. When skirmishing, not all of the light-infantry battalion's personnel need be sent forward to skirmish; some were usually held back in close formation as support to sustain the skirmishing line.

While the view of Dundas on rifles would not hold sway and battalions of riflemen were created in Britain, the French did refute their use, leading to the development of two distinct forms of capability. In Britain a training battalion for riflemen, called the Experimental Corps of Riflemen, was established in 1800 and the Baker rifle chosen as the rifle that the British Army would use officially. Along with the 43rd and 52nd regiments of Foot the men of what in January 1803 became the 95th Regiment of Foot (Rifles) underwent specialist training in skirmishing and light-infantry work. In 1805, the 95th raised a second battalion (2/95th) and a third (3/95th) in 1809. Both the 5th Battalion, 60th (Royal American) Regiment of Foot (5/60th), formed in 1798 from foreign battalions serving in the British Army, and the three battalions of the 95th would fight in the Iberian Peninsula. Rifles would also equip personnel of the KGL recruited in 1803 from Hanoverians following that territory's annexation by France. According to the historian Brendan Simms, by 1815, two KGL light-infantry battalions were exclusively equipped with rifles (Simms 2014: 7).

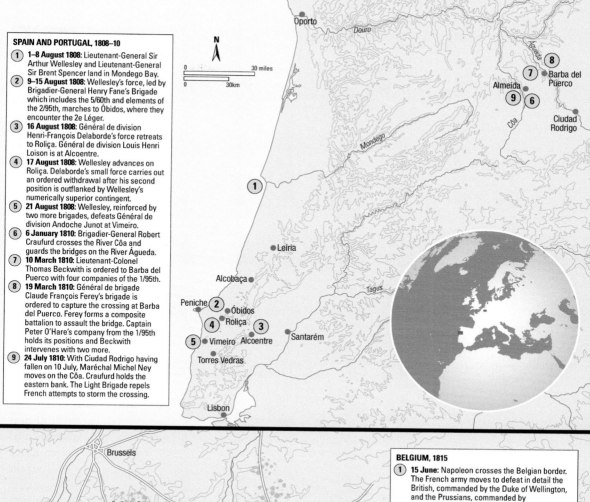

SPAIN AND PORTUGAL, 1808–10

(1) **1–8 August 1808:** Lieutenant-General Sir Arthur Wellesley and Lieutenant-General Sir Brent Spencer land in Mondego Bay.

(2) **9–15 August 1808:** Wellesley's force, led by Brigadier-General Henry Fane's Brigade which includes the 5/60th and elements of the 2/95th, marches to Óbidos, where they encounter the 2e Léger.

(3) **16 August 1808:** Général de division Henri-François Delaborde's force retreats to Roliça. Général de division Louis Henri Loison is at Alcoentre.

(4) **17 August 1808:** Wellesley advances on Roliça. Delaborde's small force carries out an ordered withdrawal after his second position is outflanked by Wellesley's numerically superior contingent.

(5) **21 August 1808:** Wellesley, reinforced by two more brigades, defeats Général de division Andoche Junot at Vimeiro.

(6) **6 January 1810:** Brigadier-General Robert Craufurd crosses the River Côa and guards the bridges on the River Águeda.

(7) **10 March 1810:** Lieutenant-Colonel Thomas Beckwith is ordered to Barba del Puerco with four companies of the 1/95th.

(8) **19 March 1810:** Général de brigade Claude François Ferey's brigade is ordered to capture the crossing at Barba del Puerco. Ferey forms a composite battalion to assault the bridge. Captain Peter O'Hare's company from the 1/95th holds its positions and Beckwith intervenes with two more.

(9) **24 July 1810:** With Ciudad Rodrigo having fallen on 10 July, Maréchal Michel Ney moves on the Côa. Craufurd holds the eastern bank. The Light Brigade repels French attempts to storm the crossing.

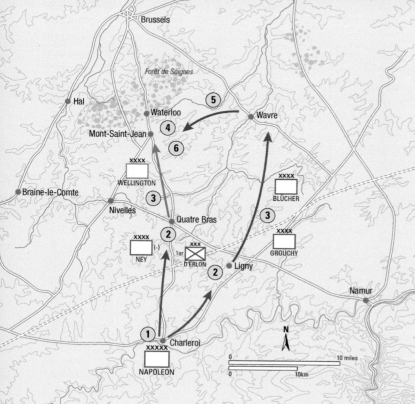

BELGIUM, 1815

(1) **15 June:** Napoleon crosses the Belgian border. The French army moves to defeat in detail the British, commanded by the Duke of Wellington, and the Prussians, commanded by Generalfeldmarschall Gebhard Leberecht von Blücher.

(2) **16 June:** Ney seizes the crossroads at Quatre Bras while Napoleon is with Maréchal Emmanuel de Grouchy defeating the Prussians at Ligny. Général de division Jean-Baptiste Drouet d'Erlon marches between both battlefields and is not committed to either battle due to a mix-up with orders.

(3) **17 June:** Instead of retreating towards Germany, Blücher heads north to Wavre and promises to move to support Wellington the next day. Wellington pulls his army back to a ridge south of Mont-Saint-Jean.

(4) **Night, 17/18 June:** The 2nd Light Battalion KGL is sent to hold the farm of La Haye Sainte in front of the ridge behind which Wellington has stationed his army.

(5) **Afternoon, 18 June:** Prussian formations brought across from Wavre make their presence felt. Napoleon needs to defeat Wellington prior to the Prussians' decisive arrival on the battlefield; the French emperor is reluctant to commit his Imperial Guard in support of a massed cavalry charge, however, and the British line holds.

(6) **18 June:** La Haye Sainte is successfully defended until early evening when, with his ammunition used up, Major Georg Baring orders a retreat. Napoleon is again reluctant to commit his Imperial Guard immediately after La Haye Sainte is captured. When the Imperial Guard infantry are thrown in, they are repelled and French morale is shattered.

The Opposing Sides

ORIGINS AND DOCTRINE

British

The British use of light infantry was heavily influenced by the British Army's experiences in the dense terrain of North America. The ambush of Major-General Edward Braddock's column in July 1755 during the French and Indian War (1754–63) and the use of rifles by French settlers prompted the creation of specialist light regiments. In Pennsylvania one-third of settlers were German; many, alongside British and Irish settlers, joined the 1st to 4th battalions of the 60th (Royal American) Regiment of Foot, which fought as light infantry though it was not officially designated as such; the regiment's training stressed aimed fire rather than massed volleys in line. At first, the soldiers of the 60th Foot were limited to service in the colonies and could not be based in Britain, except the Channel Islands and the Isle of Wight. The fighting in the Netherlands in the 1790s had shown that skirmishing tactics could also be successful in Europe; however, the British recruited foreign regiments armed with rifles on the basis that they would serve in the colonies. Events in the Iberian Peninsula from 1808 would bring such troops to mainland Europe.

Many of the foreign regiments were light-infantry units. In May 1794, Prince Charles of Lowenstein-Wertheim raised a regiment of *chasseurs* armed with rifles; they were taken into British service in January 1795 and served in the West Indies. Lowenstein also raised a regiment of fusiliers partially armed with rifles in 1796. At the same time, Baron Ferdinand von Hompesch recruited Hompesch's Light Infantry, formed of both *chasseurs* armed with rifled carbines and fusiliers armed with rifled muskets. In December 1797, losses to disease and problems recruiting replacements from Germany because of French military successes there prompted the amalgamation of the foreign

regiments on Barbados into a new battalion, the 5th Battalion, 60th (Royal American) Regiment of Foot (5/60th). Lowenstein's two regiments would provide the basis of the battalion in the West Indies. Men of Hompesch's Light Infantry on the Isle of Wight would be added later. In 1800, Lowenstein raised a regiment of light infantry, mostly Poles with German NCOs and German or French officers; after service in Egypt they were stationed on the Isle of Wight in 1802, when 300 men were also incorporated into the 5/60th.

Meanwhile, Brigadier-General John Moore, who commanded a brigade in Flanders in 1799, blamed the British failure in that campaign on the lack of skirmishers; he was not able to compete with *chasseurs* causing disruption while his battalions were carrying out manoeuvres. The French won the campaign using mixed-order infantry formations – columns and lines – preceded by skirmishers. The threat of invasion provided the catalyst to the reforms that many in the British Army had advocated. Moore was in a position of influence to have the reforms implemented. He made sure that five line-infantry regiments were trained as light infantry, always with the intention that they should be able to fight as line infantry and also be capable of skirmishing.

Separately, in 1799 Lieutenant-Colonel William Stewart, while attached to the Austrian forces allied to those of Britain, had witnessed the importance of skirmishers to French success in northern Italy and proposed that every line-infantry battalion's light-infantry company should have a platoon armed with rifles. In January 1800, Colonel Eyre Coote Manningham, a light-infantry officer who believed that a rifle regiment was needed, was sent 14 detachments from line-infantry regiments to train as riflemen. Each regiment was ordered to provide three officers and 34 men, armed at first with Prussian rifles. The personnel were supposed to be picked men, but many commanding officers offloaded their undesirables and on 22 March, 52 were returned and replacements requested. That same month, the 33 Fencible regiments in Ireland (raised to defend against invasion) were asked to provide Manningham

In 1793, the British Army relied upon German soldiers to bolster their small force of volunteer regulars fighting the French. In Flanders, the French use of skirmishers termed *tirailleurs* made the British realize that light infantry were needed. Training British light infantry would take time; hiring Germans, who were thought to be innately suited to sharpshooting, was an easier solution. In 1794, the British government paid German states to provide 20,000 soldiers; by 1795, however, peace treaties between these states and France prevented them from hiring out their soldiers to the British. Instead, the Enlistment Act of 1794 enabled the creation of regiments of foreign recruits, such as Hompesch's Light Infantry (left) the Chasseurs Britanniques (middle) and the Corsican Rangers (right). (ASKB) with 12 volunteer recruits each; the volunteers would each receive 10 guineas, a huge sum of money in 1800 when a farm labourer received 8s a week.

By August 1800, 396 recruits from the 33 Fencible regiments were on the books; 230 were Scottish, and would arrive in England from September. By then the 26 officers and 482 men from the 14 line regiments had already been formed into seven companies; six regimental detachments had embarked in July on the abortive expedition to capture Ferrol in northern Spain. The regimental detachments were ordered to re-join their regiments in October, including those sent to Ferrol, but roughly 20 per cent opted to be discharged in order to re-join Manningham's unit. By the end of 1800, bolstered by Irish recruits, Manningham had 435 NCOs and men; establishment strength was 896 officers and men. The light-infantry officer Captain Thomas Beckwith joined from the 71st Regiment of Foot on 25 August. In June 1801, 539 men went to Weymouth in Dorset where they trained during the summer. In November 1802 they marched to Moore's light-infantry camp at Shorncliffe in Kent.

The KGL would also use rifles. Formed in Britain following the disbandment of the Hanoverian Army in 1803 when France occupied Hanover, the KGL would expand in 1805 when a British expeditionary force was sent to the territory after French soldiers were withdrawn to face the Austro-Russian Army. The expedition stayed until February 1806; the KGL doubled in size to 13,300 men, being composed of ten infantry battalions – including two of light infantry – plus five cavalry regiments, artillery batteries and engineers. Losses had to be replaced, however, and recruits from various German states and Poles would supplement the original Hanoverian recruits.

In 1815, the 2nd Light Battalion KGL, stationed in Belgium, was below strength as most non-Hanoverians had been discharged after the end of the Peninsular War in April 1814; this made the unit more homogeneous and cohesive than the KGL line-infantry battalions, which retained 50 per cent of their recruits from German states other than Hanover. The 2nd Light Battalion's personnel still included plenty of nationalities, such as the Pole Alexander Dobritzky, serving in the 3rd Company, and the Fleming Baptiste Charrier, in the 5th Company. In April 1815, the number of companies was reduced from ten to six as cadres of officers and NCOs were sent to strengthen the Hanoverian Army militia. On the evening of 17 June, the 2nd Light Battalion was sent to garrison the farm of La Haye Sainte, 250yd in front of the ridge that the Duke of Wellington had chosen to defend. Two rifle companies from the 1st Light Battalion KGL would reinforce the battalion during the battle.

French

In the years before the French Revolution (1789–99), the French Army attached companies of *chasseurs* to infantry battalions to act as scouts and skirmishers. In 1759 each infantry regiment was told to pick three soldiers from each company that would be formed together in a *chasseur* company to operate in woods and built-up terrain. Those who were chosen were the best marksman. The nature of warfare during the American Revolutionary War together with the changes to the French Army wrought by the French Revolution would give decisive traction to the developing ideas about light infantry. In 1788, 12 new light-infantry battalions were established in the

In 1799, each of France's administrative divisions formed auxiliary battalions that existed to provide basic training. These auxiliary battalions formed *chasseur* companies from those personnel who were the most energetic and most likely to survive the long marches light infantrymen were asked to undertake. These companies would join light-infantry regiments. The use of skirmishers and attack columns during the French Revolutionary Wars (1792–1802) distinguished the French Army from its more inflexible and rigid enemies and won the French many battles. Soldiers were fielded in pairs to give mutual support and to ensure there was always one of them ready to give fire. Here, two re-enactors operating as skirmishers and wearing the bicorne hat issued during the French Revolutionary Wars are shown covering each other. (RADEK MICA/AFP/Getty Images)

French Army to fight the *petit guerre* ('petty war'); their service would include advance guards, reconnaissance, raids and camp security. The 1788 ordinance demanded robust men that were good marchers; however, following the French Revolution, while light-infantry *demi-brigades* were formed in 1794 by bringing together a regular light-infantry battalion with two Garde nationale battalions, by 1800 there was little difference between line- and light-infantry *demi-brigades* as they both followed the same set of instructions for firing and manoeuvring. Even so, the number of soldiers familiar with skirmishing and giving aimed fire increased as French Army formations found movement in line on many occasions to be impractical. The column was used because there was insufficient time to train the hastily raised soldiers to move around the battlefield in line. Deploying columns in open order tended to suit the rather relaxed style of discipline of the early Revolutionary units. The combination of moving and attacking in column supported by skirmishers encouraged French Army commanding officers to seek to defeat the enemy by threatening a charge rather than by using firepower in a battle of attrition.

During the 1790s, while both types of *demi-brigade* were adept at skirmishing, there was a doctrinal difference as light infantry always moved at the head of the column on the march; they were expected to march quickly, and hold ground until the line infantry arrived. Gaiters terminating below the knee were worn to give more flexibility, and coat-tails were shorter than those worn by the line infantry so they would not snag on foliage as much. The light-infantry battalion had eight *chasseur* companies along with a *carabinier* company. In each company there were three officers – a *capitaine*, a *lieutenant* and a *sous-lieutenant*. A *caporal* commanded each of eight sections. *Carabiniers*, forming the elite company, were chosen not simply on the basis of height; they were the best soldiers in the battalion.

Despite the adoption and development of the rifle within the British Army, Général de division Guillaume-Philibert Duhesme thought that the rifle was suspect because the soldier would be tempted to sit back and fire at long range; Général de division Jean-Jacques Basilien de Gassendi believed that French soldiers were temperamentally unsuited to the rifle (Urban 2003: 81). Even so, on 1 September 1813 Maréchal Jean-de-Dieu Soult wrote to the Minister of War, Henri Jacques Guillaume Clarke, noting the effectiveness of enemy riflemen (Urban 2003: 228). Losses to his officers were completely disproportionate because of the activities of the riflemen; Soult described this mode of making war as being very detrimental to the French war effort.

RECRUITMENT, MORALE AND LOGISTICS

British

On 18 January 1803, the Experimental Corps of Riflemen was redesignated the 95th Regiment of Foot (Rifles); Beckwith was promoted lieutenant-colonel and given command. On 6 May 1804, 250 privates formed a cadre for the 2/95th, which also incorporated recruits from the militia. A third battalion (3/95th) was formed in early 1809, with many officers detailed from the 1/95th. Only two of ten captains in the 1/95th who were company commanders in January 1809 were still in their positions that May; 2nd Lieutenant George Simmons was a new officer and the most junior, serving in Captain Peter O'Hare's 3rd Company. Private Robert Fairfoot from the militia was also a new soldier in the company. Other newcomers included Private Edward Costello; his section commander was Corporal Tom Plunket, a veteran of the La Coruña campaign. Both Costello and Fairfoot were enticed by stories of campaigning they heard from relatives.

This illustration depicts a Rifles officer in 1798. (ASKB)

Less appealing, at least initially, was service in the 5/60th. On 1 January 1798, the 5/60th, commanded by Lieutenant-Colonel Frederick von Schlammersdorf, was up to strength with 1,072 officers and men. Schlammersdorf died of the fever on 28 September 1798 and was replaced by Lieutenant-Colonel Baron Francis de Rottenberg, an officer from Hompesch's Light Infantry. The vast majority of recruits had military experience and were on average 26 years of age, a slightly older average than British recruits. A surprising number were in their forties, with the oldest aged 64. In January 1803, while in the West Indies, the battalion discharged 445 men because their terms of service had ended; only 59 re-enlisted, most for five years and some for ten. On their return to the Foreign Depot at Lymington in Dorset, none of those who refused to re-enlist could be persuaded to stay; there were fewer than 300 soldiers in the battalion. By 1804, of 28 officers present during an inspection, 17 were foreign (in 1798 there were no British officers); 15 were absent, on leave or had not bothered to appear. The youngest was aged 19 and the oldest, 50. Of the rank and file present, 585 were foreign; there was a single Irishman. The battalion was 232 men below strength. Most rank-and-file soldiers were aged between 25 and 35; there were 89 aged between 40 and 55, while only 71 were 20 or younger. Only 40 had served for ten years, but 218 had served for four years. There were 231 that had enlisted for life.

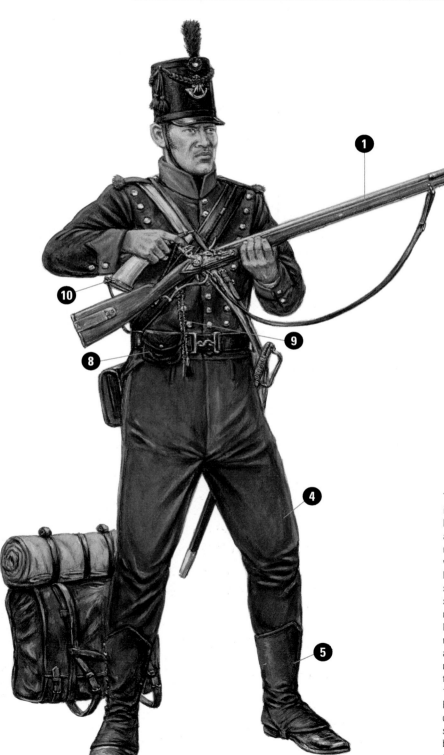

This rifleman landed in Mondego Bay at the beginning of August 1808 and from 8 August began a march south to Lisbon. He was on board ship in Cork harbour in southern Ireland since June and the expedition sailed in July, but he did not expect to be sent to the Iberian Peninsula. Following a minor skirmish on 15 August at Óbidos, his battalion rested on 16 August and then marched on Roliça on 17 August. The encounter at Roliça is his first experience of battle. He is shown skirmishing ahead of the battalion to force the French off the hill upon which the village is situated.

Weapons, dress and equipment

The 5/60th only received the Baker rifle (**1**) to replace the battalion's Prussian rifles in June 1808. Weighing 9.5lb and measuring 46in in length, the weapon was sighted for 100yd with a folding sight for 200yd and was effective up to 300yd. His sword-bayonet (**2**) hangs at his left hip.

He wears the characteristic rifle-green jacket (**3**) with regimental red facings and dark-blue breeches (**4**). His gaiters (**5**) are cut into the shape of the 'Hessian' boots associated with light troops. His headgear is the 'stovepipe' shako (**6**) retained by the British Army's rifle and light-infantry regiments throughout the period.

Each rifleman typically carried 50 loose balls in the ammunition pouch (**7**), a cleaning kit (**8**) on the belt, a picker and brush (**9**) for the touch hole and priming pan, a powder horn (**10**), a rag and tallow, a brass-wire cleanser and a small oil bottle. Riflemen initially had problems loading the rifle balls, and the regiment acquired 450 wooden mallets to help hammer them into the rifle barrel. The balls were made of soft lead to ensure they had a smooth surface that would not affect their trajectory. Many soldiers carried a mould with which to make rifle balls while on active service. A linen haversack (**11**) and water canteen (**12**) are also carried. His black knapsack with blanket (**13**) is on the ground beside him.

On 1 November 1805 the unit was still 225 soldiers below establishment, with 27 officers, 30 sergeants, 17 buglers and 522 rank and file. The battalion sailed to England that month. In December the 5/60th moved to Hilsea and then Haslar Barracks near Portsmouth in Hampshire, close to the Foreign Depot at Lymington from where the unit received new recruits. On inspection in July 1806, the battalion was 200 men below establishment, with 131 aged between 16 and 25, 428 aged between 25 and 40, and 67 aged between 40 and 50. A total of 31 personnel had served 14 years or more, 190 between seven and 14 years and 337 less than seven years. Pay was 1s a day, those with seven years' service receiving 1d extra and those with 14 years' service, 2d extra.

In September 1806, the interception of a French naval squadron heading to the West Indies resulted in the capture of men from various French regiments. The 26e Ligne included German-speakers from Mainz, while the 66e Ligne incorporated Flemish-speakers from Belgium. In early October, 100 prisoners-of-war were recruited from these units; some were *voltigeurs* with light-infantry skills. The conditions in some of the prisoner-of-war camps were hard and encouraged many to volunteer. With these additions, the 5/60th was up to strength by the end of the year and moved to Kent in May 1807. Rather than being transported to the campaign in Denmark, however, they went to Cork in southern Ireland. The establishment increased to 1,000 when 214 new recruits arrived from the Foreign Depot.

The Foreign Depot at Lymington served all the foreign regiments. Agents based at ports could send foreign recruits to Lymington and receive payment for their trouble. Two officers were in Germany recruiting. There was a depot in Strålsund, a Swedish territory in the Baltic (this depot moved to Gothenburg in Sweden when French forces took Strålsund in 1807), and staff based in Schleswig Holstein in Denmark, to administer the process. Other nations also sought out Germans who wanted to fight; recruiters discovered that British service, with the prospect of sea travel and disease-ridden postings in the West Indies, was not as popular. By 1807, following Napoleon's defeat of Prussia, the supply of recruits from Strålsund had dried up. The emphasis now was on the retention of existing soldiers and recruitment from prisoners-of-war.

The practice of recruiting foreigners had many detractors, and critics decried the policy of seeking prisoners-of-war to join the British ranks. While the riflemen of the 5/60th succeeded in establishing a good reputation on the battlefield, the battalion's existence would be debated following a spate of desertions during Moore's Spanish expedition. The experience of the 5/60th in 1808–09 gave the unit's commanders cause for concern as the battalion suffered desertions of soldiers who had previously served in the French Army. Nearly one in eight soldiers of the battalion would desert or attempt to desert by the end of 1808. The deserters were not German-speaking soldiers from Général de division Andoche Junot's army who had surrendered and were waiting to be sent back to France; Brigadier-General Francis de Rottenberg, who helped establish Hompesch's Light Infantry and wrote manuals used in the training of riflemen for British service, had told the battalion commander, Major William Davy, to recruit from these men. Davy wrote to Lieutenant-General Sir Hew Dalrymple, Commander of the Portuguese Expedition, via Lieutenant-General Sir Arthur Wellesley and initially his suggestion did not receive a favourable reception. When Dalrymple was replaced, however, either Moore or Lieutenant-General Sir Harry Burrard (Dalrymple's deputy) gave Davy permission to recruit from the foreign soldiers. Two hundred Swiss *voltigeurs* were recruited, but went to the 2/60th and were sent to the West Indies. The soldiers who deserted were from those Frenchmen recruited during the autumn of 1806 from prisoner-of-war camps on the south coast of England.

The desertions occurred in October 1808 when Moore marched through heavy autumn rains. Davy, at the head of five companies going through Ciudad Rodrigo, reached Salamanca on 16 November but would go no further. He was ordered to escort the sick and baggage back to Portugal. From October to December, Davy had only seven deserters he could not find but Major William Woodgate, on a route further south, had 75. This had prompted the order to send both detachments back. Moore recommended that the 5/60th was so bad that it should be disbanded, and if not, sent to the colonies. The 5/60th received orders to go to Cádiz in January 1809; however, Moore's defeat meant that every battalion was needed in Portugal and so the battalion stayed there. Davy was told to send back the recruits that were taken from prison ships and prisoner-of-war camps; in total, 154 men, including 110 deserters, some of whom were experienced men, were sent back to Britain in March 1809; 56 invalids also returned with them. Davy informed the officers that he trusted in their zeal to enforce discipline in order to ensure desertion at these levels did not occur again.

In June 1810, General De Merck, a Belgian formerly in French service, sought to recruit Germans from prisoners-of-war held in Spain; he ended up recruiting French and Italians, too. Colonel Lewis von Mosheim, commander of the Foreign Depot at Lymington, complained in 1811 that of 575 recruits shipped from Gibraltar, 350 were French. Few of these Frenchmen would serve with the 5/60th, however. Mosheim wrote to Lieutenant-Colonel Edward Williams, the commanding officer of the 5/60th, to tell him that three French sergeants were going to be sent to his battalion and were to keep their rank (Griffith 2019: 176). Williams was worried by this and Mosheim had to reassure him that he had carefully chosen the men in question. In 1812 Mosheim wrote that he had 159 men ready to be transported to the battalion, carefully selected, and he was in no doubt they would give satisfaction. Ensuring that clothing and provisions were provided was important to keep the men in the ranks. With such measures, discipline was restored and the battalion provided reliable service during the rest of the Peninsular War.

The recruits were needed as the companies were often below official establishment. In early 1812, the 6th Company of the 5/60th had a lieutenant, five sergeants, four corporals, one bugler and 27 privates; there were three

As the Peninsular War progressed, more British infantry battalions would be given training as skirmishers and the habit of forming composite light-infantry battalions from the light companies of line battalions was gradually eschewed; such improvised units could not compete with the self-confidence of specialist formations from the Light Division or the rifle battalions. Often, riflemen would operate together with light-infantry soldiers. Here, a rifleman of the 95th is shown in 1807. (ASKB)

men with 18–20 years of service, seven with 14–17 years and eight with 7–13 years. Two of the men were aged 55 or older and ten between 45 and 54, and only two were younger than 25. By October 1812, the company had 39 privates, with more of the men in their twenties.

In July 1809, both KGL light-infantry battalions joined the British expedition to destroy French ships and port facilities in the Scheldt Estuary. Antwerp was not taken, and by the end of the year they returned to England with nearly 50 per cent sick with fever. The light-infantry battalions were not deployed to the Iberian Peninsula until 1811, when both were with Brigadier-General William Beresford in the south near Badajoz. Although the 2nd Light Battalion KGL did not take part in the siege of Badajoz, on 22 July 1812 the battalion deployed as skirmishers at the battle of Salamanca, and with cavalry in support stormed a hill held by the French.

The other ranks of the KGL perceived themselves not as mercenaries but as loyal subjects with a deep hatred of Napoleon's treatment of Germans. They had no respect for the Hanoverians who were serving in Napoleon's Hanoverian Legion. Lieutenant Emmanuel Biedermann, an officer in the 2nd Light Battalion KGL who fought at Waterloo, fought in what he believed to be wars of liberation to throw off French tyranny (Simms 2014: 10).

During the Peninsular campaign, life was hard, with a diet lacking in protein and minerals. Germans had a reputation for making the most of what they were given, however, and they carried various ingredients in order to make their meals more palatable. The men of the 5/60th were also good at plundering and had to be supervised while in camp to ensure they were not absent out foraging without orders. If caught, offenders could expect numerous lashes as punishment. The need to maintain patrols, travel lighter, and often camp rough made a rifleman's life harder than that of the line infantryman. Shelters were made out of branches or brushwood. Tents were not issued to the rank and file until 1813, and exposure to the elements often led to sickness. The average march rate was 15 miles per day. Sickness was the biggest killer, with a long journey to reach a hospital in one of the few wagons allocated to the task. Despite the poor hygiene, many of the sick would stay in hospital as long as they could rather than return to their battalion. During their recovery, officers were billeted in private houses and were visited by medical staff. They would be forced to return to the regiment if they did not attend medical boards tasked with assessing their fitness.

French

In 1798, a French law established compulsory military service for unmarried males aged between 20 and 25. A lottery was used to determine who would be called up to fulfil each region's quota. In later years, conscripts were borrowed from earlier classes and teenagers started to join the ranks. Recruits would serve for four years or the duration of the conflict. A medical examination would determine if they were fit for duty and many tried to feign injury. Except in Paris, substitutes could be purchased, but the fee was not affordable for 95 per cent of the population. In the regiment's depot battalion, recruits were given their uniforms and underwent basic training up to platoon manoeuvres prior to being sent out to one of the field battalions. Sometimes, basic training was done en route to the field battalions. Regimental medical personnel could refuse recruits and send them back; but this hardly ever happened, and it was more likely that a frail recruit would be kept back at the depot and exercised. Target practice at the depot was rare; there were some competitions organized by officers for money to distract from the tedium, but few rounds were expended at the target. At the depot, the new recruits could encounter returning wounded personnel and hear tales of atrocities in the Iberian Peninsula.

There were volunteers into the French Army; these men had a choice of the regiment in which they would serve, perhaps the unit of a relative or family friend who could offer preferment. Alternatively, a volunteer could join the *vélites* of the Imperial Guard where he could be expected to be commissioned in four years, or enrol in the military academy to train to be an officer by paying 1,200 francs per year. With graduation approaching, cadets were asked to name their preferred choices. Cadet Faré wanted to join the light infantry; there, a junior officer could employ his knowledge and distinguish himself most easily (Crowdy 2002: 17). Often detached from his company, the junior light-infantry officer was in sole command and if he performed some dazzling feat he would be seen as being personally responsible. He would always be the first into battle. A line-infantry officer, unhappily in position behind his soldiers, commanded nothing but himself and shared the danger of every common soldier; however, with little family influence, Faré was sent to serve in a line regiment. Young officers from the academy were not always popular when they arrived at their battalion; every cadet that graduated prevented a sergeant-major from receiving a commission. Affairs of honour often led to duels. If an officer from another regiment insulted an officer, his colleagues might demand that he ask for a duel.

Service opportunities with the light infantry increased when a new *voltigeur* company was established in each light regiment in March 1804 and in each line regiment in March 1805. The March 1800 law that set 1.624m (5ft 4in) as the recruit's minimum height did not apply to *voltigeurs*; they had to be less than 1.597m (5ft 3in). Recruits previously classed as unfit could now become elite soldiers, enjoying higher pay. Initially, *voltigeur* companies were not filled with experienced soldiers because there were not sufficient numbers of men of such height in the regiments; however, they needed to be strong, agile men capable of firing accurately and with speed. They carried the dragoon musket, while officers had rifled carbines. Cornets replaced the line infantry's drums.

Losses in the 1805–07 campaigns were high. The 9ᵉ Léger suffered 466 dead and 1,000 personnel were discharged due to wounds or desertion; 28 NCOs were promoted to officer. Even so, in February 1808, regiments were expanded from three to five battalions each, including the depot battalion. Three of the seven companies of *chasseurs* in each battalion were disbanded;

A rifle-armed soldier of the light company of a KGL line-infantry battalion. Unusually, some KGL line-infantry battalions fielded riflemen, with the majority carrying the usual smoothbore musket. During the Peninsular War, the majority of the personnel of the 1st and 2nd Light battalions KGL were also armed with the musket, with only a minority carrying the rifle (Fosten 1982: 38; Chappell 2000a: 43). According to Simms, the light company of the 5th Line Battalion KGL at La Haye Sainte was armed with muskets (Simms 2014: 46), but a few rifles may have been fielded by the company. The KGL light-infantry battalions never completely used British drill regulations or the English language. German remained in use in the 2nd Light Battalion KGL, with English employed during sentry duty and on parade. German officers took English lessons and were soon fluent. Relations between officers and the rank and file were closer than in most British battalions. British officers were not from notably wealthy backgrounds because commissions in the KGL were cheaper than in other regiments. (ASKB)

This *voltigeur's* battalion was sent to the Iberian Peninsula in October 1807 and marched into Portugal by the end of the year. He witnessed the civil uprising in Portugal that happened in the spring of 1808 and was initially deployed north with Loison; however, he was forced into Almeida and had to march south where he joined Delaborde's division, which was sent to delay Wellesley's march on Lisbon. He has seen Wellesley's columns deploy to outflank his position near Roliça, but he knows that a stronger position on the hills south of the village will serve as good cover to delay the British.

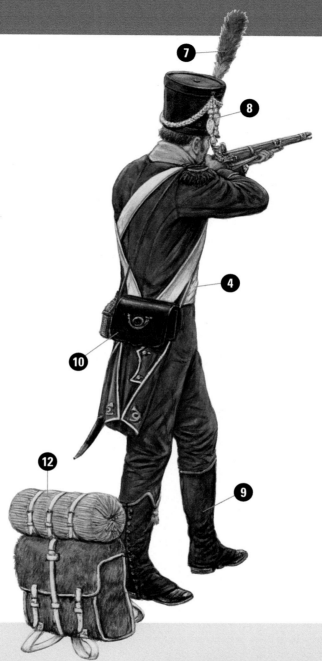

Weapons, dress and equipment

He is armed with a Charleville Year IX Dragoon musket (**1**), 3.9in shorter than the Charleville musket issued to the fusiliers, *chasseurs* and grenadiers. Soldiers of elite companies carried the *sabre-briquet* ('lighter sabre') with company-colour knot (**2**), carried in a combined frog with the bayonet.

Skirmishers needed to be dressed appropriately in order that they could move with ease. By 1808, this man's regiment had replaced the short-tailed jacket of the early Empire with a longer-tailed *habit* (**3**), but retained the characteristic pointed lapels; the white waistcoat (**4**) was worn in summer. Fringed epaulettes (**5**) denote his elite status,

as do the yellow collar (**6**) and shako plume (**7**). The diagonal cords (**8**) on his shako are distinctive of the 2ᵉ Léger. His gaiters (**9**) are cut to resemble light-cavalry boots.

The *giberne* (cartridge box; **10**) had two compartments that had 15 cartridges each. The cartridge had a lead ball weighing 0.95oz and 0.44oz of gunpowder. An external pouch contained rags for cleaning, a screw, a ball extractor, spare flints, lead envelopes and practice wooden flint. As with all parts of the French Army, he carries a privately purchased water canteen (**11**). He has removed his haversack with attached greatcoat (**12**) in order to achieve a better aim.

those companies that remained were each increased to 123 rank and file, including two drummers or cornetists. The *voltigeur* and *carabinier* companies remained, and the number of officers did not change. *Carabiniers* had to have four years of service or have participated in two campaigns. These measures were implemented during the summer of 1808.

Many of the French regiments sent to the Iberian Peninsula in 1808 were provisional regiments composed of depot battalions (which had no elite companies) or were hastily built that year. The depot of the 9e Léger included as many as 200 Italians who would join the Spanish Army when the battalion surrendered after Général de division Pierre Dupont's defeat at Bailén in July 1808. With the depot wasted in this fashion, the expansion of the regiment into four field battalions was held up. The 9e Léger had a third field battalion by mid-1808, but setting up a fourth field battalion was delayed. In March 1809, recruits had no time to train at the depot and did this on the march. Of the 18 officers in the companies of the 3/9e Léger, 12 were newly promoted.

The 3/2e Léger fought the 5/60th in Portugal in 1808; the regiment (then designated a *demi-brigade*) was formed in 1796 and was in Egypt during 1798–1801. In 1803, the unit deployed to the English Channel as part of the French invasion force. In May 1804, the regiment formed three *voltigeur* companies; the *carabiniers* were detached to form elite battalions, which fought in the Austrian campaign in 1805 alongside those of other regiments. In January 1806, the 2e Léger minus its *carabiniers* was in France and the Netherlands. In October, the 1/2e Léger and the 2/2e Léger were sent to participate in the Prussian campaign; the 3/2e Léger was initially kept in Paris and only mobilized in August 1807, to be part of Junot's army that would head to the Iberian Peninsula. That October, the 3/2e Léger (with the 3/4e Léger) formed the 1er Régiment provisoire d'infanterie légère in Général de division Louis Henri Loison's 2e Division. Loison was sent to the River Douro in June 1808 and ended up in Almeida. He marched to Lisbon in July and was posted to Évora. The two light-infantry battalions were detached and given to Général de division Henri-François Delaborde. In June 1808, the three other field battalions of the 2e Léger would also be ordered to Spain. Each of these battalions included only 500 men because of the rapid expansion that had just occurred.

Général de brigade Claude François Ferey's brigade, which fought the 1/95th on the River Águeda in March 1810, was composed of the 2/32e Léger, three battalions of the 66e Ligne and four battalions of the 82e Ligne. The 32e Léger was established in 1805 from Ligurian (Genoese) soldiers; the 2/32e Léger was the depot battalion, which was formed in Grenoble in 1806 and moved to Toulon that October. In August 1807, the battalion was with Loison's division. After defeat by Wellesley in August 1808, the unit was repatriated to France in late September. Transferred to 6e Corps in July 1809, the 2/32e Léger was in Ferey's brigade that was part of Loison's division.

The 66e Demi-brigade d'infanterie de ligne was formed of three volunteer militia battalions in 1796. They were sent to Guadeloupe in 1802. The 66e Ligne was formed in 1804 by reorganizing the two battalions of the 66e Demi-brigade in Guadeloupe; the depot was at La Rochelle. The 3/66e and 4/66e were formed in France and were part of Junot's 3e Division in 1807. They were repatriated; the 4/66e, together with two new battalions (5/66e and

6/66ᵉ), was sent to the Iberian Peninsula in 1809 where the battalion served in Ferey's brigade.

The 82ᵉ Demi-brigade d'infanterie de ligne was formed in Rennes in 1796 primarily from a *demi-brigade de bataille* that had returned from the French colony of Saint-Domingue on the Caribbean island of Hispaniola. In 1801, Napoleon designated two battalions to serve in the West Indies along with the 66ᵉ Ligne and the 26ᵉ Ligne. The 3/82ᵉ and the depot stayed in France; the 4/82ᵉ was formed and with the 3/82ᵉ went to join Junot's 3ᵉ Division in 1808, fighting at Vimeiro on 21 August and losing 100 killed including a battalion commander, and 200 taken prisoner. At that battle, the *voltigeurs* and grenadiers were formed into an elite regiment with other such companies. The two battalions were amalgamated into the 4/82ᵉ on their repatriation to France when only ten officers and 280 men disembarked in late October; in 1809 this battalion was renumbered the 6/82ᵉ. A new 4/82ᵉ and 5/82ᵉ were formed in 1809 and would join the 6/82ᵉ in Galicia in 1810. The 7/82ᵉ followed as part of a second reserve division. The regiment gathered near Valladolid. Many of the men were sick, with 1,000 in hospital. In March 1810, the regiment was part of Ferey's brigade. That April, the 4/82ᵉ had 20 officers and 652 men, while the 5/82ᵉ had 17 officers and 507 men and the 7/82ᵉ mustered nine officers and 276 men. The 6/82ᵉ was better off, with only 77 sick, but in June the regiment still had only 1,795 men. The elite companies were formed, together with others in Ferey's brigade, into a composite battalion to attack British forces on the east side of the River Côa in July 1810. Ferey recommended Lieutenant Thévenard, a *voltigeur* company commander, to receive the Légion d'honneur because his approach to the river was conducted with skill and bravery.

WEAPONS, TRAINING AND TACTICS

British

Major Patrick Ferguson had fought in the American Revolutionary War and experienced the effect of rifles in the hands of the Americans. Massed volleys did not work when columns were ambushed in close terrain. The Americans used fire and manoeuvre in small groups to harry the British, wearing clothes that blended in with the terrain. Officers mounted on horses made prominent targets and columns of men strung out on the march through thick forest could lose cohesion when officers were no longer present. They had no formal training in how to handle ambushes or combat dispersed groups making full use of cover. Independent groups of rangers to protect colonists from the indigenous population were set up in the 1750s and these units were expanded during wartime. The men were encouraged to show initiative when their officers were debilitated. By 1771, a light company was given to every line-infantry regiment; but training was deficient as experience had already been lost.

In 1776, Ferguson exhibited a breech-loading rifle he invented to Field Marshal Lord Townshend, Master General of the Ordnance. In the presence of King George III, he fired nine shots; he found the bull's-eye with five and was within an inch with the other four at 100yd. He fired three rounds lying on his back and six while standing. Ferguson volunteered for service in North America where he was tasked by the commander-in-chief there, General Sir William Howe, with forming a corps of riflemen from volunteers from the regiments stationed there. At the battle of Brandywine on 11 September 1777, Ferguson kept the enemy at bay effectively; when he was wounded, however, his men were disbanded and the rifles returned to storage. By 1780, Ferguson was in charge of 300 American Loyalists named 'Ferguson's Sharpshooters'. While campaigning in South Carolina against soldiers similarly equipped he was ambushed and his column wiped out by vastly superior forces. Other rifle formations in North America included the *Jäger* companies from various German principalities. In 1785, Oberstleutnant Johann von Ewald, formerly a *Jäger* company commander, wrote *Essay on Partisan Warfare*, a treatise on the use of light infantry that would form the basis for Rottenberg's work.

Rottenberg's *Regulations for the Exercise of Riflemen and Light Infantry, and Instructions for their Conduct in the Field* formed the core of the riflemen's training material. Dundas had written *Rules and Regulations for the Formations, Field-exercise, and Movements of His Majesty's Forces* to facilitate fighting in close order as ordinary infantry when needed. The movements and drills specific to riflemen that were to be carried out were specified in Rottenberg's work (quoted in Cusick 2013: 74–75). Rottenberg specified that when in skirmish order, each file of two men would operate in pairs, making sure one man always had his weapon loaded. To deploy from close order, a company of two platoons in eight sections would first deploy a section from each platoon forward 50yd, then another section from both platoons would advance 110yd and extend. The remainder should be kept back in reserve. If line infantry were in support, the entire company could go forward in extended order. They could be used to cover a wide area of ground, with three half-platoons extending 50 paces (42yd) forward of a half-platoon kept in close order; pairs of files would then extend 10 paces (8yd) from each other. When firing, the man on the front right of the pair of files would take three paces forward and shoot, with the other three advancing to fire in succession.

The Light Brigade would be a protective screen for the whole army; it could deploy a tactical skirmishing screen ahead of the main body to harry the French and keep their *voltigeurs* at bay until the moment of battle. The men of the Light Brigade also served to hide the dispositions of the main army. When deployed as the advance guard of a march column, a rifle company would split into four half-platoons; the first would be 500 paces (416yd) ahead of the main force, the second 200 paces (166yd) forward of the first, with a sergeant and six men detached 100 paces (83yd) further on. The third and fourth half-platoons would position 300 paces (250yd) to either side of the first platoon, with a sergeant and six men 100 paces (83yd) further out. The company would be in arrow formation. Distances would vary according to terrain and weather. No impassable objects were allowed to get between the unit components. Rearguards were to be formed in a similar formation in reverse. Patrols of a sergeant with a section would form up with front and flank guards in a similar formation.

When encountering a village with no warning of the enemy's presence, a few men were to be sent forward to bring back two civilians for separate questioning to determine whether they were telling the truth. The purpose was to collect intelligence rather than fight the enemy if he was found to be in superior numbers. Forming pickets around the camp was another primary duty that needed to appreciate the terrain to work out likely enemy avenues of approach. A picket at night should vacate the area occupied during the day in order to trick the enemy. A few men detached to the flanks would be able to open an effective fire if the main picket was attacked. In cold weather where fires were needed, the positions of the pickets were to be changed and the fires left burning to attract the enemy to the wrong location. Rottenberg recommended that an officer share the privations with his men and not take shelter. Small patrols were to be sent out to prevent the picket from being surprised. The expectation was that riflemen would spend most of their time in small sections using fieldcraft to protect the main army.

François Jarry, who had served in the French Army before 1789 while teaching at the École militaire, also wrote instructions for light infantry and pointed out that the French would have sharpshooters concealed in terrain that needed to be dislodged by their British counterparts. Light infantry needed to gather information about the enemy in terrain where the cavalry could not operate. Riflemen were so important that Jarry envisaged them to be the rearguard of the rearguard. He outlined the importance of patrolling to seize prisoners-of-war to question them, even to escort a staff officer to discover the purpose and location of an enemy force. He placed even greater emphasis upon the use of pickets and patrols than did Rottenberg.

Front and rear views of a rifleman in 1800. Riflemen used either a prepared cartridge, composed of a ball and powder bound together in a paper tube covered in beeswax, or a loose ball with a greased patch. With a prepared cartridge the riflemen poured some gunpowder from the paper tube into the muzzle of the barrel, then inserted the ball and then the cartridge paper. He used the ramrod to make a tight fit. Cartridges were supposed to be used only in an emergency. Most of the time, greased patches made from linen and kept in a compartment in the rifle butt were used. Fine-grained gunpowder was poured from the powder horn onto the priming pan. The rifleman judged how much gunpowder was needed depending on the range, but this was difficult if the gunpowder was damp because this increased the gunpowder's weight, making estimating the amount required difficult. (ASKB)

Lowenstein's men originally used some of the 5,000 Prussian M1787 *Füsilier-Schützengewehr* rifles purchased by the Board of Ordnance in 1798; each was about the same length as a musket and had to be loaded while standing. Shorter rifled carbines were also in British use in small numbers; these could be reloaded while kneeling or prone. In early 1800, the Board of Ordnance tested various British-made rifles and the Baker rifle – a copy of the German rifled carbine by master gunsmith Ezekiel Baker – was chosen. The 95th started to receive Baker rifles in 1803, the 5/60th in 1808.

The riflemen could load their weapons either with loose powder and ball or – more rapidly – with prepared cartridges. For aimed fire, loose gunpowder would be poured from a powder horn and the ball would be wrapped in a cloth patch to help fit it tightly into the rifling. Cartridges had gunpowder that was shaken into the pan and were envisaged by Rottenberg to be used only in close order, an instance that he thought would very seldom occur; in the Iberian Peninsula, however, loading with cartridges was the norm despite their availability being the same as that of the patched ball. Using loose gunpowder and a patched ball, three rounds could be fired in 1 minute 55 seconds. Using cartridges and unpatched balls, this took 1 minute 10 seconds but with a loss in accuracy; using cartridges and patched balls took 1 minute 30 seconds, with a slight loss in accuracy. Rottenberg ensured that soldiers were given a large target with which to practise to ascertain the accuracy of their aim. Soldiers should be proficient at 200yd, with the best shots competent at 300yd.

Riflemen were ordered to fire independently rather than in massed volleys, when targets presented themselves, and from all positions – standing, sitting, prone and kneeling – in order to exploit cover. They practised firing at moving targets at various ranges and snap targets that appeared fleetingly. Sergeants carried the rifle instead of the line infantry's spontoon and many junior officers also preferred to do likewise as the rifle made them less obvious targets. Target competitions were organized and prizes given. There were three classes of rifleman: a black leather cockade worn above the bugle-horn badge was given to the lowest (first class), while a white plume was given to second-class shots, and a green plume to the highest (third class). Brass and silver medals of merit were awarded for high standards of proficiency and meritorious service and hung from white and green ribbons on the chest. Each company had two platoons and each platoon two half-platoons or sections; a sergeant assisted by a corporal commanded each section. Each section had a soldier of merit who would take command of the section if both NCOs were casualties. These were named chosen men and corporals were appointed from among them.

The Hanoverian soldier Friedrich Lindau, who served with the KGL, described encountering French *voltigeurs* in March 1812. The French skirmishers did not relish fighting the KGL riflemen, owing to the superior range of the rifle; the poor quality of the French muskets and ammunition compounded this disparity in range and accuracy. Moreover, the German riflemen were able to load and fire their rifles while lying down (Lindau 2009: 72). In this illustration first published *c.*1805, Baker shows that a rifle could be fired while lying on the ground. (ASKB)

French

In 1793, light-infantry tactics were widely used because French recruits did not have the training required to carry out more complicated manoeuvres. Whole battalions could be sent to skirmish; however, the usefulness of keeping a reserve was rapidly realized as cavalry could inflict terrible damage on soldiers in skirmish order. Skirmishers were taught to refrain from firing until their fire could be effective. Indeed, their deployment from the advancing battalion would be delayed until the last possible moment to prevent the enemy from throwing out their own skirmishers to delay or disrupt the advance. When the column was about to close with the enemy, skirmishers would retire through the intervals between the battalions; if this was difficult to do, they would lie flat instead, or move to threaten the enemy flank if this was close by.

The training of a French light infantryman took four months; during this time the recruit was trained in arms drill, loading and platoon manoeuvres. He was taken on progressively longer route marches to harden him physically. At the field battalion, formation changes were taught and battalion manoeuvres were practised. Once battalions were deemed proficient, divisional manoeuvres were carried out.

Because skirmishers needed to shoot at individual targets on horseback and enemy light infantry who were attempting to use cover, target practice was a priority. In his 1804 work on light-infantry tactics, the French military theorist Colonel Guyard specified that the skirmisher needed to be trained to use the correct amount of gunpowder to fire his musket ball the required distance. Each man needed to trust his weapon and keep his composure. Light infantrymen were taught to guard the camp in a village or wood and to conduct patrols. They were instructed to patrol ahead or on the flanks while a column moved in close terrain in order to warn of the presence of the enemy. While guarding a river line, positions were not to be exposed to fire; redans could be built, even for sentries, if the earth was too hard to dig entrenchments. The main position could be in a nearby village that was out of artillery range; cavalry should be placed on the flanks.

There were few formal French instructions on how to skirmish. The French military thinker Colonel Étienne Alexandre Bardin did not support formal systems of skirmishing, instead suggesting that because the signals could sometimes not be heard on the battlefield, every skirmisher needed to decide himself when and where to deploy. In 1805, Duhesme wrote orders to *voltigeur* officers specifying how they should manoeuvre their men. In skirmish order, each regiment's three *voltigeur* companies should deploy at least two-thirds of their men forward, with the rest kept in close order in reserve. Duhesme ordered them to target enemy gunners in particular. The skirmishers would be co-ordinated by a single officer. If the enemy attacked with a superior force the skirmishers would retreat through the intervals between the battalions and protect the artillery.

Maréchal Louis-Nicolas Davout suggested that a *capitaine* of a skirmishing company should take his men 200yd ahead of the formation he was covering and that he split them into three platoons. The *capitaine* would command the platoon in the middle and with him would be the *sergent-major*, two *sergents*, two *caporaux* and the majority of the drummers or cornetists. The *capitaine* was to send men to reinforce the other two platoons as needed. *Lieutenants* commanded these two platoons and they would take their men 100yd to the left and the right of the centre platoon and in front. The *lieutenant* commanding the right-hand platoon would order the first two ranks to have their files face to the left and start marching, stopping a file every 15yd. The *sous-lieutenant* would do the same in reverse with the platoon on the left. The two platoons would meet ahead of the centre platoon. The men would then face the front. The third rank of each platoon would stay behind and form a reserve.

The skirmish files would then advance 100yd in front of their reserve. This skirmish line could be deployed in a skirmish column to cover a flank on the march. If attacked, the column would face outwards to the threat and deploy perpendicular to the marching column they were covering. In this instance the *capitaine* would have a much smaller third section and take them to the flank most in danger.

In an ambush, the preferred tactic was to send some men to outflank the ambushers. If the enemy were in a village, the two *lieutenants* would take up positions with their escorts on good routes in and out and then send in their skirmishers to clear the buildings. The *capitaine* would stay outside. When a

village was known to have enemy inside it, the buildings in the flanks or at the back would be immediately attacked by the two *lieutenants'* detachments; the *capitaine* would attack the centre with the reserve when the enemy had committed his own reserves.

COMMAND AND CONTROL

British

Officers could purchase promotion or be given higher rank through seniority; but the system was corrupt, with many commissions being bestowed through political patronage. Reforms in 1794 helped: there was an increase in the number of free commissions and lieutenants could not be promoted captain without at least two years' experience, while more senior officers needed six years. A military college and cadet school were created. When a vacancy occurred, the most senior officer would be given a chance to purchase; if he could not afford to do so, then the next most senior officer would be given the opportunity. Vacancies arising from a death were usually filled on seniority alone without purchase. Patronage could also secure a promotion without purchase. The demand for officers was high and the supply of those able to purchase commissions could not keep pace. New commissions were invariably given without purchase and the majority of the 5/60th's sergeant-majors would go on to gain a commission; there were already too many captains and majors, however, and promotion was slow. The long-standing service and vast experience of the captains would benefit the companies that often were asked to operate independently from the battalion.

Officer training was based on the assumption that company commanders were given a degree of latitude and independence, as companies were to be able to operate separately. Company commanders were expected to use their own initiative to provide each other with mutual support if needed. They often served on the staff and lieutenants could command companies. Words of command were replaced by bugle calls, but sometimes these could be misheard on the battlefield. Officers and NCOs also had whistles to communicate orders. The ethos was that self-reliance was the result of knowledge and every officer needed to be an expert trainer. Officers had an interest in the welfare of their men because they were given responsibility for them.

The riflemen were in part relied upon to operate in dispersed order because their intelligence and initiative were brought to the fore; in British light-infantry companies there was in theory an extra lieutenant, sergeant and corporal, however, as those not so motivated could use the distance that deploying in open order gave to lie low or slip away. The use of supports behind the skirmishing line further discouraged such practices and gave the light-infantry commanders the ability to reinforce the skirmishing line or replace tired soldiers who had exhausted their ammunition. If threatened by cavalry, skirmishers could retire on the supports that were already closer together to give a better chance of driving the cavalry off. If deployed as individual companies to support a brigade, the men of the 5/60th would rely on a composite battalion of light companies from the brigade to be their supports; the 95th could use the battalions of the 43rd and 52nd Light Infantry regiments, while the 1st and 2nd Light battalions of the KGL were brigaded together.

At the beginning of 1808, Rottenberg departed the 5/60th to train light infantry in Kent. A former captain in the unit, Major William Woodgate, arrived to take charge of the battalion. Another former captain, Major William Davy, arrived in March having purchased his majority in February ahead of 13 more senior captains. By April, there were eight lieutenants who needed to be appointed; Captain John Gailiffe was appointed brevet major. Some officers applied for commissions because overseas service would likely lead to promotion opportunities. In March 1808, Ensign John Joyce wrote a letter, termed a memorial, outlining his character and experience, seeking promotion to lieutenant. He had 15 years' experience, most with the Royal Irish Artillery, being commissioned in the regiment as ensign in July 1807 through recommendation by Rottenberg. Joyce waited until October 1809 for his promotion without purchase.

In a letter of June 1808, Davy pointed out the lack of lieutenants and noted that two captains, three lieutenants and one ensign were on detached duty. Sergeant-Major Matthew Fürst was promoted ensign

Moyle Sherer, a light-company officer in the 2/34th Foot at the battle of Vitoria on 21 June 1813, thought that 'The English do not skirmish so well as the Germans or the French; and it is really hard work to make them preserve their proper extended order, cover themselves, and not throw away their fire; and, in the performance of this duty, an officer is, I think, far more exposed than in line fighting' (Sherer 1824: 59). The rifle officer's distinctive uniform is depicted in this contemporary German illustration. (ASKB)

on 23 June. Many companies on campaign in the later years of the Peninsular War would have only one officer. In addition, language barriers could be problematic in the German battalions – most British officers had limited German and NCOs and rank and file had limited English. Detached service could hamper the ability of the unit staff to attend to administrative issues.

In the 1/95th, most officers had not purchased their commissions and were professional soldiers in search of a fortune. O'Hare had secured promotion since 1800 by seniority alone; he could not afford purchase. To his soldiers, O'Hare appeared to be a coarse character with no manners who was certainly no gentleman; when his boots were stolen by a soldier, O'Hare had the man flogged. Simmons had eight siblings and was not from a rich background; he sent £20–30 of his £160 salary home to his parents. The 1/95th had 33 lieutenants and ensigns. Simmons was given a commission as he persuaded many soldiers of his militia regiment to follow him into the battalion.

Captain Jonathan Leach, 2nd Company commander, had transferred from the 2/95th. In 1809, Leach described Brigadier-General Robert Craufurd, the commander of the Light Brigade, as tyrannical. While Craufurd would have a man flogged if he fell out of the ranks because of exhaustion, Beckwith developed a system whereby the tired soldier would give others his pack and weapon while he recovered. When the battalion was in camp, Craufurd would order the men to wear full kit and take their weapon on the daily march to the river to bathe; Beckwith ordered them to wear forage caps and take a stick instead. In the summer of 1809, the 1/95th lost a company's worth of men because of the fever. Costello and Fairfoot were both ill; they pulled through, however, and went with O'Hare into Spain in January 1810. When the battalion was on the Águeda, Beckwith relaxed discipline in order that the soldiers would follow him when he needed them most.

French

The indiscipline, insubordination and lack of theoretical and practical training often seen among French troops during the French Revolutionary Wars were not tolerated in the campaigns after 1804. During an inspection of the 9e Léger in 1802, Général de division Adolphe Éduard Mortier noticed that the men had to lean back to get a cartridge and that the sabre scabbard interfered with their stride when the soldier moved. Some of these issues were still not attended to when another inspection occurred the following year. The captains were not checking their men's kit and dress sufficiently prior to the inspection; in the campaigns after 1804, however, officers were more stringent with standards as the earlier Revolutionary fervour was on the wane.

Promotions to fill officer vacancies were often done in-house and informed by seniority rather than merit. Older and incapacitated captains could be packed off to the depot to allow younger officers promotion. Rather than an internal appointee, however, in 1803 the 9e Léger received a new 33-year-old *colonel*, Claude Marie Meunier, to shake things up. The

This British officer wears the overcoat and the post-1812 'Belgic' shako with false front, indicating that he is serving in the light company of a line-infantry battalion. Harry Ross-Lewin, who served as a junior officer in the 1/32nd Foot in the Iberian Peninsula, highlighted how British officers would encourage their men not to take cover as this seemed to be cowardly – a notion Ross-Lewin thought was absurd. The Germans of the rifle company from the 5/60th that he operated with were 'always dodging from tree to tree or ensconcing themselves between rock and fences, with admirable method and steadiness, while the British skirmishers would step out sturdily on the open space, and make a target of himself for the enemy' (Ross-Lewin 1904: 305–06). The British troops he was referring to were from light-infantry companies from line battalions rather than the light-infantry regiments. (ASKB)

previous commanding officer, Mathieu Labassée, was a professional officer from the *ancien régime*; the new commander was a volunteer who in 1792 had been chosen by his peers to be an officer and had served in Napoleon's Foot Guides in 1799.

Each company had a *capitaine*, *lieutenant* and *sous-lieutenant*. An officer needed to be able to read the terrain and decide where to site his troops; if he was able to discern this with clarity, he would inspire his men. During a retreat, companies needed to be at the correct distance to offer support to each other; and the commander had to keep detachments on his flanks to ensure enemy cavalry did not make their presence felt. The successful officer needed to pay attention to natural cover that could be used by his own troops or those of the enemy. He also needed to assess the strengths and weaknesses of enemy positions and to appreciate where enemy reserves might appear. Skirmishers were given orders either by their officers shouting or the sound of a drum or cornet telling them to advance, move right, move left, fire or retire. With drums, however, there was the potential for a mix-up with the main column if they were ordering a movement that did not apply to the skirmishers. The *capitaine* had to keep the skirmish line within sight at all times and would detach men from his platoon to do so if his sight lines were intermittently interrupted. An NCO from the *capitaine*'s platoon could be sent to relay orders verbally.

Roliça

17 August 1808

BACKGROUND TO BATTLE

Following the end of the war between France and Russia in July 1807, five companies of the 1/95th and five companies of the 2/95th embarked for Copenhagen to seize the Danish fleet. They were part of an infantry brigade that also included the 1/43rd and 2/52nd Light Infantry regiments. A cavalry brigade and three other infantry brigades accompanied them, commanded by Major-General Sir Arthur Wellesley. Copenhagen was bombarded during August and September and the Danish fleet surrendered to spare further shelling of the city. The rifles guaranteed the security of the artillery batteries.

Napoleon was furious at this British seizure of the Danish fleet and demanded that Portugal declare war on Britain. Portugal refused and instead entered into a defensive treaty with Britain. Napoleon believed that the British force that had besieged Copenhagen would be sent to Portugal and ordered the occupation of Portugal in October 1807. Northern Portugal would be given to Spain to guarantee Spanish assistance to the French occupying forces. Owing to contrary winds, an 8,000-strong British force commanded by Lieutenant-General Sir John Moore and ordered to make its way from Sicily to Lisbon, only reached Gibraltar on 8 December, too late to arrive in Lisbon prior to French forces entering the Portuguese capital. Moore sailed back to Britain and with 12,000 men and three companies from the 1/95th would be sent to Sweden in April 1808. The Swedish king was not co-operative, however, and Moore's command would return to England in July.

By early 1808, the Spanish agreed to let Napoleon send 40,000 soldiers into Spain to support the French forces in Portugal; he soon sent double this number. Maréchal Joachim-Napoléon Murat with 25,000 men was in Madrid when on 2 May an uprising led to 1,000 French soldiers being killed or wounded. Murat retaliated and brutally suppressed the rebellion. Napoleon persuaded Carlos IV, King of Spain to abdicate on 19 March and installed his brother Joseph-Napoléon Bonaparte on the throne on 2 July as José I. Spain was already in the grip of revolt in most regions, but the Spanish Army, deprived of 15,000 soldiers that Napoleon had persuaded the king to send to Germany, was widely scattered and ineffective, with 20,000 soldiers in Galicia and 25,000 in Andalusia. Napoleon had amassed 110,000 soldiers in the Iberian Peninsula. He wanted to seize the ports of Valencia and Cádiz, but the small French forces sent to both suffered defeats at the hands of the Spanish; most significantly, Dupont's two divisions surrendered at Bailén on 19 July, prompting the French evacuation of Madrid. On 14 July, Général de division Jean-Baptiste Bessières managed to defeat a Spanish army at Medina de Rioseco further north, but his communications with Junot were fraught.

In May 1808, a 5,000-strong force led by Wellesley, who had been promoted to lieutenant-general on 25 April, was assembled in Cork. The rebellion in Madrid was followed by a popular uprising in Portugal in June, which persuaded the British government to send Wellesley to the Iberian Peninsula. In early July Wellesley's force, including four companies (446 officers and men) of the 2/95th commanded by Major Robert Travers and the 5/60th, sailed for the Iberian Peninsula; two brigades from Harwich in Essex and Ramsgate in Kent would follow. Moore would be sent too after returning from Sweden.

The revolt in Portugal had liberated the north of the country. A French force commanded by Loison sent to capture Oporto was driven back by sheer weight of numbers. Loison was surrounded in Almeida, but some of the French garrison escaped and headed to Lisbon. They reached Santarém and united with other French forces. The 3/2ᵉ Léger was sent to Óbidos, the 3/4ᵉ Léger to Santarém, the 4ᵉ Suisse to Peniche and the 32ᵉ Ligne to Abrantes. Countering the rising in Évora was the main priority for the French and they needed to capture the city to preserve communications with France. Loison took Évora on 29 July and carried out massacres that gave him a reputation for cruelty.

On 20 July, Wellesley arrived in La Coruña. The Spanish were not keen on having him there and with the Portuguese uprising in progress, he decided to make his way to Oporto and land to the south of the city in Mondego Bay. He ordered Lieutenant-General Sir Brent Spencer with 5,000 men on Gibraltar to join him. Wellesley knew Junot had detached Loison with 7,000 men to Évora. On 26 July the British transports were in Mondego Bay; however, a heavy swell delayed the landing until 1 August when the boats started to take 8,700 men ashore. The process of landing took five days.

The rifles were part of Brigadier-General Henry Fane's Brigade, which was the first to land and pushed on 6 miles through hot sand and then pitched camp near Lavos. They would be the advance guard when the army started to move. On 5 August, Spencer's 5,000 men arrived and took three days to land. Wellesley also had 380 cavalry from the 20th Light Dragoons and,

In this late-Victorian illustration by Major R.A. Wymer, a rifleman is shown loading his rifle. In the summer of 1806, five companies of the 1/95th and three companies of the 2/95th were sent to South America to recapture Buenos Aires in Argentina. In July 1807, they were ambushed in the narrow city streets; ten officers and 219 men were killed or wounded out of 24 officers and 580 men present. In January 1808, they returned to Shorncliffe Camp and the 2/95th and the 5/60th were part of Wellesley's expedition that was about to be sent to South America. (ASKB)

once Spencer arrived, five 9-pdrs, 14 6-pdrs and five mortars. On 7 August, five men from the 5/60th deserted, including Private Francis Marschefsky, a veteran who had joined in 1799.

On 9 August, the army moved off with Fane and some Light Dragoons in the lead; because of the lack of transport, the tents were left behind and the baggage was still on board ship. The men suffered from the intense heat and a lack of water. Heathland and pinewoods were traversed. Tracks with high hedgerows shut out cooling breezes. On 10 August, the advance resumed with 200 riflemen and some dragoons as the advance guard. Leiria was captured when deserters reported the French were no longer there.

Wellesley was made aware that more reinforcements were to be sent out; when they arrived, he was to be superseded by Dalrymple with Burrard as Dalrymple's deputy. On 12 August, 6,000 Portuguese commanded by Marechal de Campo Gomes Freire arrived; he refused to accompany Wellesley, but provided some 1,500 men to join him. On 14 August, the army reached Alcobaça where it camped with Fane's Brigade guarding the camp. The march carried on to Caldas da Rainha on 15 August. Wellesley wanted the walled town of Óbidos captured that afternoon.

On 1 August, Junot had received news that Wellesley was landing and had ordered Loison back from near Badajoz. On 6 August, he sent Delaborde from Lisbon with 2,500 men to delay Wellesley in an effort to buy time in which to consolidate the scattered French forces. On 10 August, Delaborde was at Alcobaça where he was joined by three battalions. With perhaps 4,350 men (Général de brigade Paul Thiebault, Junot's chief-of-staff, claimed 1,900 men were in the ranks; Colonel Maximilien Foy, a divisional commander in the Iberian Peninsula, 2,500) organized into two battalions of light infantry (the 3/2e Léger and the 3/4e Léger), two battalions of line infantry (the 1/70e Ligne and the 2/70e Ligne), a battalion of Swiss infantry, the 26e Chasseurs à cheval and five guns, Delaborde pushed on to Batalha; here the position was too wooded for a defence and he withdrew to Óbidos where he left a rearguard and then went 3 miles south with the rest of his force to Roliça with some men stationed on high ground 2 miles in front. Three companies of the 70^e Ligne were detached to Bombarral and Cadaval. Delaborde had already detached six companies of Swiss soldiers to Peniche. Now he hoped to delay Wellesley until Loison reached him. Loison was in Abrantes on 9 August, but had to stop for two days because his men were exhausted. On 13 August he was at Santarém; again he had to stop, and he would not be in Alcoentre, 15 miles east of Óbidos, until the evening of 16 August.

On 15 August, Travers was ordered to take four rifle companies and dislodge elements of the 2e Léger from Óbidos. Captain Hercules Pakenham's 4th Company of the 2/95th and three companies from the 5/60th were sent out. They received fire from the town and, moving south, pushed eagerly forward ahead of the army; but French cavalry and the rest of the 3/2e Léger, forming the rearguard, forced them to retire. Travers began a fighting withdrawal and Spencer, hearing the fighting, advanced to assist him with an infantry brigade. Pakenham was slightly wounded, three riflemen were killed, one was missing and two were wounded from the 2/95th. The 5/60th had one killed, five wounded (two later died of their wounds) and 17

Grenadier et Fusilier du 9ne Reg: des Chasseur à pié.

A *carabinier* and *chasseur* of the 9e Léger in the full-dress uniforms worn at the beginning of the Peninsular War. Some French light-infantry regiments wore the white waistcoat. (ASKB)

missing (ten of these soon returned). Wellesley castigated their imprudence while pushing forward. Óbidos was captured on 16 August. The army stayed there that day and waited for supplies, giving Loison another day to reach Delaborde.

On the morning of 17 August, because he had a strongly superior force, Wellesley decided to launch a pincer attack on the first French position. There were three roads south of Óbidos and Major-General Ronald Ferguson with two brigades of infantry and three companies of the 5/60th would use the eastern road to guard against Loison appearing. The Portuguese, commanded by Lieutenant-Colonel Nicholas Trant, had the western road and Wellesley, with four brigades of infantry and two artillery batteries, the centre road.

1   15 August: Major Robert Travers with four rifle companies is ordered to dislodge the French from Óbidos. Captain Hercules Pakenham's 4th Company of the 2/95th and three companies from the 5/60th are sent out in front. Elements of the 2e Léger ambush them and Travers carries out a fighting withdrawal.

2   16 August: Lieutenant-General Sir Arthur Wellesley captures Óbidos and waits at the town to receive supplies. Général de division Henri-François Delaborde takes position behind a slope near Roliça.

3   0700hrs, 17 August: Wellesley decides to envelop the French position. Major-General Ronald Ferguson, with two brigades of infantry, moves along the eastern road to guard against Loison appearing. Wellesley, with four brigades of infantry and two artillery batteries, has the centre road. The 5/60th and the 2/95th are in extended formation to cover the 1–1.5 miles to Ferguson's column.

4   Morning, 17 August: Delaborde's *voltigeurs* engage the riflemen; with the cover this provides, the main French force withdraws to the second position 1 mile to the south.

5   Afternoon, 17 August: Brigadier-General Henry Fane's riflemen pursue the *voltigeurs* to the second position.

6   Afternoon, 17 August: Seeing the riflemen's advance and thinking that the envelopment has started, Lieutenant-Colonel George Lake, commanding officer of the 29th Foot, advances up a gully in support of his battalion's detached light company; Lake's battalion uses the adjacent gully to that used by the light infantrymen, however.

7   Afternoon, 17 August: French skirmishers fire at Lake as he attempts to form line. He is shot and killed. The rest of the 29th Foot reaches the top and Delaborde begins a counter-attack.

8   Late afternoon, 17 August: Wellesley orders a general advance to relieve the 29th Foot. Fane moves his riflemen up the ridge, and the 1/5th Foot and 1/9th Foot advance to the crest.

9   1630hrs, 17 August: With Ferguson's brigades appearing on his flank, Delaborde orders a general retreat, covered by his cavalry, through the village of Zambujeira. Three of Delaborde's guns are lost here.

Battlefield environment

At Roliça, seven companies of the 5/60th and ten companies of the 2/95th would advance on the flank of the main attack up a gully and would initially be thrown back before eventually (with the French right threatened by envelopment) reaching the ridge. The British advanced south along a valley, flanked by hills and with a line of hills at the end. Delaborde took up his first position on the hill at Roliça, some way in front of the ridge at the end of the valley, with the intention of retreating to a second line as soon as the British threatened Roliça.

The terrain certainly suited open-order fighting for both sides. Situated in thick brushwood and high heath, the French light infantry could keep up an invisible and destructive fire as the riflemen advanced. Delaborde held high ground, thick with scrub, 100ft above the plain where the valley narrowed to less than 1 mile, to compel the British to deploy. The French second position was protected by ravines on both flanks, and by a steep hillside cut up by gullies.

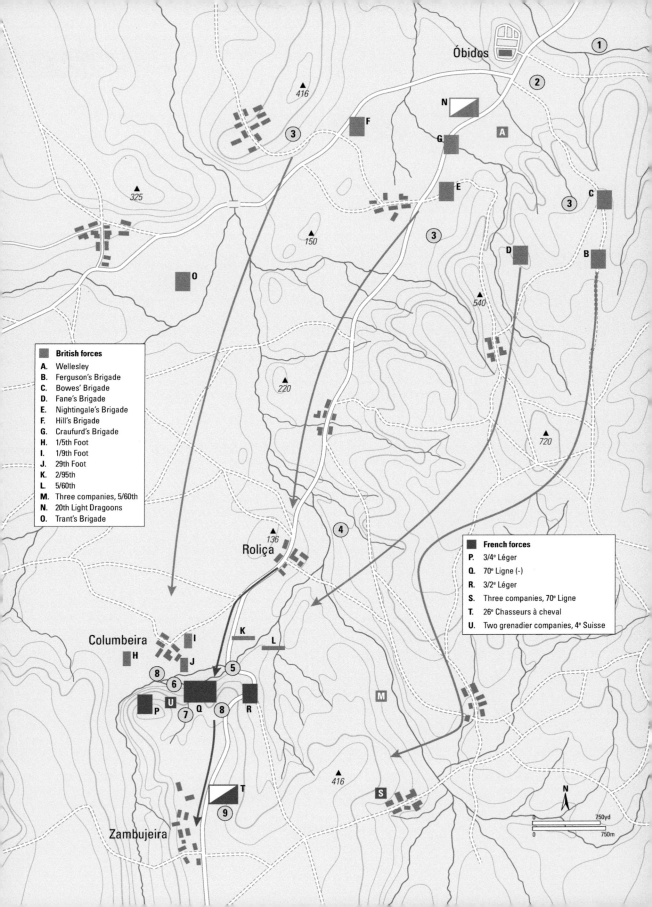

Óbidos

416

325

① ② N ▨ Ⓐ

F G ③ C

E ③ B

D

540

O

220

150

720

British forces

A. Wellesley
B. Ferguson's Brigade
C. Bowes' Brigade
D. Fane's Brigade
E. Nightingale's Brigade
F. Hill's Brigade
G. Craufurd's Brigade
H. 1/5th Foot
I. 1/9th Foot
J. 29th Foot
K. 2/95th
L. 5/60th
M. Three companies, 5/60th
N. 20th Light Dragoons
O. Trant's Brigade

136

④

Roliça

French forces

P. 3/4e Léger
Q. 70e Ligne (-)
R. 3/2e Léger
S. Three companies, 70e Ligne
T. 26e Chasseurs à cheval
U. Two grenadier companies, 4e Suisse

Columbeira

I

H

K

L

J

⑧

⑤

⑥

P U Q ⑧ R

⑦

M

416

S

T

⑨

Zambujeira

N

0   750yd
0   750m

INTO COMBAT

At 0700hrs on 17 August, the British movement started with Fane on Wellesley's left in extended order to cover the 1–1.5 miles to Ferguson. Wellesley's brigades slowly started to approach Roliça; they stopped to dress their line, which was being disordered by broken ground. On nearing the French line, the rifles formed into a long skirmishing line and reached the hills on the French right. Delaborde's *voltigeurs* were engaging the riflemen and with this protection the main French force withdrew to the second position 1 mile to the south behind the village of Columbeira, where Delaborde intended to make a more resolute stand. The position was 500ft above the plain, a stream guarded the left flank, and there were steep and broken spurs rising up to the ridge that created narrow gullies. Bare rock protruded from the scrub and high heath and firs were scattered about. The hill sides were steep and cut up with enclosures.

Wellesley sent Ferguson and Trant on enveloping moves again prior to a vigorous attack on the French front. He organized his four brigades in order to make demonstrations against the four gullies while the enveloping forces moved forward. In the easternmost gully, Fane's Brigade would be supported by the 1/45th Foot; in the next gully, the 82nd Foot would advance; in the next, the 29th Foot and 1/9th Foot would deploy; and in the westernmost gully, the 1/5th Foot would operate with the light companies of the 1/9th, 29th and 82nd Foot.

Fane's riflemen had pursued the *voltigeurs* to the second position; seeing the riflemen's advance, Lieutenant-Colonel George Lake, the commanding officer of the 29th Foot, thought the envelopment had started. From his position in the centre, Lake decided to advance his battalion up the slope. Lake's was the first battalion to reach the foot of the gully as other battalions were delayed while they crossed streams and went around villages; Lake's men were fired at by the French as they were the closest. Encouraged by his grenadiers, Lake launched his battalion up the steep gully. He already had deployed his light company with those of the 1/5th Foot and the 82nd Foot to skirmish in a gully to his right. The sides of the gully helped cover the British from the fire of the French. Halfway up, the British took off their packs. At the top, with the battalion's light company not immediately available, Lake started to form line, waiting for the other four companies. Lake's men apparently fraternized with some Swiss from two grenadier companies that were with Delaborde; this was a ruse, however, and the 70ᵉ Ligne attacked the 29th Foot in the flank.

The French were firing from behind a low stone wall. Lake was targeted by skirmishers and his horse was shot. The rest of the line companies were still making their way up the gully. Lake mounted a spare horse and was making an effort to straighten the line when a skirmisher shot him. Lake was killed and 40 of his men were taken prisoner, including six officers. The British companies withdrew and found the other companies advancing. The 29th Foot rallied and, when Wellesley ordered a general advance by the 1/5th Foot and Fane's Brigade, started to advance with the 1/9th Foot. The Swiss grenadiers reportedly resisted gallantly, losing 37 killed and 27 wounded. Situated on the eastern side by the road, Fane's riflemen could exchange fire without incurring heavy casualties because they were in a more dispersed formation.

On the morning of 17 August, Wellesley decided to launch a pincer attack on the first French position. He would attack up the centre with most of his infantry. Ferguson would attack to the east and Trant, with his Portuguese troops, to the west. At the moment this pincer movement began to threaten the French position, Delaborde ordered his men back to the second position. Here, Wellesley is shown ordering forward the 1/9th Foot to support the 29th Foot, which was ambushed when it reached the top of a gully. (The Print Collector/Print Collector/Getty Images)

Wellesley intended to launch a pincer attack on the second French position, but before the flank attacks could get into place, part of his centre was engaged in the fighting. Two hours of bloody British attacks followed, each being repulsed, before finally the British were able to gain a lodgement at the top of the ridge. This is an engraving from an original painting by Abraham Cooper (1787–1868). (Hulton Archive/Getty Images)

On three occasions, Delaborde launched counter-attacks on the British as they emerged from the gullies and reached the crest of the hill, while the British were in some disorder having climbed the slope. Then Ferguson appeared on Delaborde's flank and Delaborde decided to withdraw at 1630hrs. His four battalions with two Swiss companies retired in pairs alternately, covered by his small force of cavalry. The French cavalry made repeated charges and the riflemen brought many down, including their commanding officer. One mile behind the position, the scattered village of Zambujeira lay in a defile. Here, three French guns were lost and many of the wounded were taken prisoner. The French losses were 600 killed or wounded, including Delaborde wounded. British losses were 71 killed (including four officers), 20 officers and 315 men wounded, and four officers and 68 men missing. Loison was three hours away in Cercal.

Of Wellesley's force, only 4½ battalions were involved; of these, one-third were riflemen. The 2/95th had a sergeant and 16 men killed, and three officers, three NCOs and 30 men wounded. The 5/60th had eight men killed, including Caspar Spaling, a former French prisoner-of-war, three officers and 39 men wounded (two died later) and 16 men missing of whom ten returned. Wellesley did not pursue, because he needed to cover the landing of reinforcements in Maceira Bay. He made sure each of his brigades would have a company of riflemen from the 5/60th.

Wellesley commended the French on their counter-attacks. Leach of the 2/95th described how the French on the first hill lay at the top of the slope in the heath and kept up a hot and persistent fire on them (Griffith 2019: 154–55). On the next hill, the French were again concealed and kept up a galling fire as the 2/95th ascended. The French crossed a valley and went into a wood on the other side where they were reinforced and started a withering fire on the riflemen. Having accepted the offer of a drink, Leach had another officer's canteen to his mouth when a round hit the hand of the officer, wounding him. Heath and scrub hid the French; every gully had to be cleared. The riflemen experienced heavy fire from two nearby houses; one rifleman, having had enough, decided to leap over the wall they were pinned behind and encouraged others to do the same. They dashed towards the houses and the *voltigeurs* inside decided to retreat rather than wait for the riflemen to reach them.

On 15 August, Junot had left Lisbon; he joined Loison two days later and then met Delaborde after the battle. Two roads led to Lisbon; unsure which route Wellesley would take, Junot stayed put at Torres Vedras. On 20 August he heard the British were on the road that led to Vimeiro and he moved on the village with 10,300 infantry, 2,000 cavalry and 700 gunners. That night he marched 10 miles and was within 4 miles of Wellesley by dawn. Wellesley was on the Vimeiro road because he had received news of the arrival of the two brigades sent to reinforce him. He ordered the brigades to be disembarked at the River Maceira near Vimeiro; most of their men were landed on 19 and 20 August. With these brigades were two companies of the 1/95th, commanded by Beckwith. Wellesley had 16,312 infantry, 240 cavalry and three batteries of guns with 1,500 Portuguese in support; Burrard decided not to land and so Wellesley stayed in command. Junot had a numerical disadvantage, but decided to attack the next day, 21 August. He would naively launch an envelopment on the right wing through terrain that was not suited to rapid manoeuvre. He weakened his centre to strengthen the envelopment, but still threw his centre into the attack.

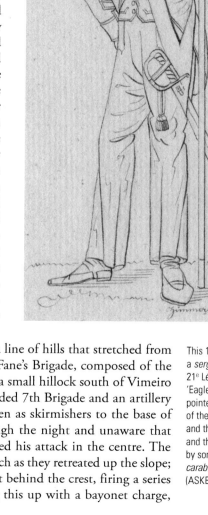

This 1808 illustration depicts a *sergent-major* of the 21e Léger with regimental 'Eagle' standard. Note the pointed lapels, characteristic of the light-infantry regiments and their cavalry counterparts, and the bearskin cap, worn by some light-infantry *carabiniers* and colour-parties. (ASKB)

Wellesley had placed his brigades along a line of hills that stretched from the north to the south-west. In the centre, Fane's Brigade, composed of the rifles supported by the 1/50th Foot, was on a small hillock south of Vimeiro covered with thick scrub with the newly landed 7th Brigade and an artillery battery. Fane deployed nearly all the riflemen as skirmishers to the base of the hill when Junot, having marched through the night and unaware that Wellesley had received reinforcements, started his attack in the centre. The riflemen were pushed back, firing at the French as they retreated up the slope; however, the intervention of the 1/50th Foot behind the crest, firing a series of volleys at close range and then following this up with a bayonet charge,

Lieutenant Charles Leslie, an officer in the 29th Foot, noticed how the German skirmishers at Vimeiro demonstrated their ability to take advantage of the ground. Fane observed one of them successfully hitting one or two French officers that were exposed in front while leading their men. Fane was so excited that he offered the rifleman half a doubloon for every other officer he hit. Here, the battlefield is depicted in this engraving after an 1812 painting by Henri Leveque (1769–1832). (ASKB)

routed the French brigade. The 7th Brigade enjoyed similar success against another French brigade that had attacked in echelon nearby. Junot then launched four grenadier battalions against Vimeiro in two attacks. In bitter fighting, the 2/43rd Light Infantry forced the French columns out of the village during the second attack.

During the battle, three British brigades were not engaged and, following the repulse of the two flanking French brigades, could have launched a pursuit, but by now Burrard had assumed command and prevented them from doing so. Dalrymple soon followed him and assumed command on 22 August. The 2/95th had casualties of nearly 25 per cent: three sergeants and 34 men killed, and four officers, three sergeants and 40 men wounded. The 5/60th had 14 killed and two officers and 23 men wounded. Total British losses were 135 officers and men killed, 534 officers and men wounded and 51 officers and men missing.

After the battle the two companies of the 1/95th were transferred to Fane's Brigade where they joined the 2/95th companies. On 28 August, some of Moore's force started to disembark in Maceira Bay, including three companies of the 1/95th. Lisbon was reached on 3 September. Dalrymple then agreed to the Convention of Cintra, which stipulated that Junot's army would be returned to France aboard British ships. Moore arrived in early October; because of government disgust at the Convention of Cintra, Dalrymple, Burrard and Wellesley were ordered back to Britain to explain why the French were permitted to return to France with their weapons.

Barba del Puerco

20 March 1810

BACKGROUND TO BATTLE

The companies from the 95th that fought at Vimeiro were soon reinforced. On 26 October 1808, four companies from the 2/95th and five companies from the 1/95th, part of a force of 12,000 men, arrived at La Coruña; Moore advanced to Salamanca in early November and by 20 December he had 25,000 men. Napoleon had entered Spain with 100,000 veterans, and on 4 December was in Madrid. Moore decided to attack Napoleon's communications by moving on Burgos; by so doing he would distract the French from Lisbon and southern Spain. Moore formed a Light Brigade commanded by Brigadier-General Sir Robert Craufurd with eight companies (750 men) of the 2/95th, the 1/43rd Light Infantry and the 2/52nd Light Infantry. The 700 men of the 1/95th were with the Reserve Division.

On 23 December, Moore heard that Napoleon with 80,000 men had departed Madrid to intercept him and set in motion the retreat to La Coruña. On 28 December, three companies of the 2/95th held the bridge across the River Esla near Benavente and defended engineers who destroyed the structure from the attentions of dismounted French cavalry. Craufurd was detached to Vigo in case Moore needed to embark there instead of at La Coruña. On 3 January 1809, the 1/95th, still with Moore, had four of its companies at Cacabelos on the French side of the River Côa; some French dragoons caught two companies covering the withdrawal across the river and one-third of the riflemen were soon casualties. *Voltigeurs* arrived, forded the river with the help of horses and engaged Moore's rearguard, but the British main body had already made good its escape and the army would embark at La Coruña on 16 January 1809. Three hundred

On 14 January 1809, the British army began to embark at La Coruña. Moore had lost 5,000 men on his retreat and stood with 15,000 men to repel the French closing in on the city. On 16 January, during the battle of La Coruña, Beckwith's riflemen – 750 men covering half a mile of front – nearly succeeded in capturing a battery of French artillery. Some French light infantry arrived just in time to drive them off. Beckwith's casualties were 45 killed or wounded. During the campaign, the 1/95th lost about 210 men killed, wounded or captured. Many of the wounded died on the voyage home. Here, a book illustration from 1910 depicts the British retreat. (The Print Collector/Print Collector/Getty Images)

and fifty men were needed to make up for losses suffered by both rifle battalions; 1,350 volunteered because of the regiment's reputation, and this surge meant that a third battalion could be formed. On 25 May 1809, the 1/95th embarked for Portugal with the Light Brigade; they arrived too late to participate at the battle of Talavera on 27–28 July. Meanwhile, the 2/95th deployed on the failed Walcheren expedition to capture Antwerp and would not recover from the losses suffered due to fever until early the following year.

In January 1810, Viscount Wellington (as Wellesley was known following his elevation to the peerage in September 1809) gave instructions to Craufurd to maintain a line in front of the River Côa with his Light Brigade unless the French appeared to be intent on a serious invasion of Portugal with a large force. He was ordered to retire on supporting divisions if this was the case. The rest of the army was on the River Mondego with Major-General Rowland Hill on the River Tagus. Wellington was worried that his initial letter might persuade Craufurd to retire too early and wrote again saying Craufurd should withdraw only if faced with so formidable a force as to manifest a serious intention of invading Portugal. A third letter on 8 March spoke of Wellington's wish to be able to assemble the army on the Côa, if it should be necessary. He did not want to withdraw from the Côa without being able to discern the enemy's strength and intentions. Holding the Côa gave time to assemble the rest of the army once these were known. The 1/95th had brought 1,100 men to Portugal in mid-1809, but malaria had caused many casualties during the autumn. By April 1810 the 1/95th would have 800 men, re-organized into eight companies.

Wellington decided to increase the Light Brigade to a Light Division, which would provide a vanguard to keep the French skirmishers away from the Anglo-Portuguese main body until battle commenced and hide the dispositions of Wellington's army. Two Portuguese battalions, the 1° and 3ª Caçadores, plus the 1st Hussars KGL, two light-dragoon regiments and a battery of horse artillery with six guns would join the Light Brigade to make up this division; however, the Portuguese would not be ready until April.

Maréchal André Masséna was given command of the Army of Portugal. By early 1810, he had been reinforced to invade Portugal and had 83,000 men in three corps, including Ney's that included Loison's division. Wellington had 25,000 British soldiers on the Portuguese border near Ciudad Rodrigo and 30,000 Portuguese regulars. Craufurd had to assess whether Masséna, if he moved to the Côa, was intent on a serious invasion of Portugal. From the Côa to the Águeda was 15 miles, with Ciudad Rodrigo in the north. The rivers flowed into the River Douro. There were four bridges spanning the Águeda, at Ciudad Rodrigo, Navasfrías, Villar and Barba del Puerco, and there were many fords when the river was not in flood. In between the two rivers lay scrubland, woodland, farms and small villages.

On 6 January, Craufurd crossed the Côa; deep snow covered the landscape. The pickets the riflemen set up frequently changed position so they could familiarize themselves with the paths and tracks. They set up a system of signalling beacons to give warning of any French approach. Craufurd placed cavalry vedettes to monitor fords and gather information about enemy movements. On 27 February, Captain Jasper Creagh's rifle company was ordered to Barba del Puerco; Creagh sent out a patrol from Bouza that found 200 French infantry and cavalry in the village. The British withdrew to Bouza and then Creagh went to Escarigo to join with two other rifle companies. With these three companies the riflemen approached Barba del Puerco and found that the French had plundered the village and then gone back across the river. A party of riflemen went to the bridge and established a picket there. They were told that the French were at San Felices de los Gallegos, 4 miles further on.

Craufurd withdrew the three companies and only decided on 8 March that he needed to have a permanent force at Barba del Puerco; however, on 9 March the French moved forward with infantry and 150 cavalry and captured the village that morning. Although they were foraging for supplies with no intention of staying, this was enough to convince Craufurd to send four companies to the village and O'Hare's company was sent to guard the bridge. The 1st Hussars KGL maintained patrols of fording sites along the river and monitored the water level; the 1/43rd and 1/52nd Light Infantry were further back near the Côa to provide support if necessary. In addition, four companies of the 1/95th were sent to Villar de Ciervos on the right, 6 miles south of Barba del Puerco; one company went to Escalhão, 12 miles on the left, near the Douro Valley, and another to Almofala. The Light Brigade had a front of 40 miles to guard.

MAP KEY

1   Night, 19/20 March: Captain Peter O'Hare's 3rd Company of the 1/95th is in place to defend the crossing of the River Águeda that is half a mile from Barba del Puerco. Lieutenant-Colonel Thomas Beckwith, with three companies, is in the village. Lieutenant James Mercer is in a tent up the slope, as O'Hare is sick and is in the village; 40 soldiers are in a chapel a few hundred yards from the bridge.

2   Night, 19/20 March: Mercer stations Sergeant Tuttle Betts' section 50yd from the bridge. Betts sends Privates Maher and McCain 15yd from the bridge.

3   Night, 19/20 March: Having marched throughout the day in a rainstorm with a composite battalion of *voltigeurs* and grenadiers leading and three line-infantry battalions following, Général de brigade Claude François Ferey reaches the slope above the northern bank of the river.

4   0030hrs, 20 March: 200 soldiers from the French composite battalion advance towards the bridge. Maher and McCain are bayoneted or taken prisoner. A warning shot is probably fired and Betts' section starts firing as the French climb the slope.

5   0030hrs, 20 March: Betts is shot and wounded. His section withdraws up the slope. Mercer sends Lieutenant Alexander Coane to the village to warn Beckwith and O'Hare.

6   0030hrs, 20 March: Mercer is shot in the head. Lieutenant George Simmons is now in charge. A desperate firefight ensues. The riflemen are harder to identify because of their dark uniforms. The white cross-belts of the French make them an easier target.

7   0100hrs, 20 March: O'Hare, situated at the top of the slope, notices the French still climbing up from the bridge. He rallies his company and his men maintain positions on the slope and keep up their firing.

8   0105hrs, 20 March: Beckwith appears with two companies of riflemen and immediately launches a bayonet charge that routs the French across the bridge.

9   0115hrs, 20 March: The French composite battalion is back on the northern bank and the three French line-infantry battalions give covering fire. Ferey decides to retreat.

Battlefield environment

In the spring of 1810, Craufurd was watching the line of the River Águeda to observe Masséna. Most of Craufurd's infantry were pulled back from the river, but four companies of Beckwith's 1/95th were close to the river, watching the bridge by Barba del Puerco (north-west of Ciudad Rodrigo). This was a strong position in a difficult pass, and Craufurd felt that the rifles would be able to hold off any force small enough to surprise them. Masséna was intent on capturing the city from the Spanish and would soon approach the river to start his push into Portugal.

The Águeda plunged furiously through a steep-sided ravine strewn with rocks and caused an unceasing noise. The bridge over the river was 100yd long and 5yd wide. The night was dark and stormy with occasional rain and this made the noise of the river louder than normal. The moon at intervals shone brightly between the clouds. The white cross-belts of the French gave the riflemen a target for their fire. The riflemen in comparison were not so distinguishable in the darkness.

The action at Barba del Puerco

British view: The section of riflemen commanded by Sergeant Betts from Captain O'Hare's company of the 1/95th is firing as the French, having crossed the bridge at Barba del Puerco that spanned the River Águeda, begin to ascend the steep-sided slope of the river valley towards the British positions. Privates Maher and McCain, two soldiers from Betts' section who were stationed nearer the bridge, are either bayoneted or taken prisoner. Betts might have heard a warning shot fired by the sentries. In the moonlight, the riflemen see the white cross-belts the French wear on top of their coats. Further up the slope, Lieutenant Mercer in his tent is being roused by the commotion. He will send Lieutenant Coane to obtain reinforcements from the village; however, they will take at least 30 minutes to arrive.

French view: *Voltigeurs* and grenadiers from Général de brigade Ferey's command have crossed the bridge at Barba del Puerco without being spotted because the noise of the gushing water made their approach hard to hear. They have neutralized the two sentries and have begun to climb the path that winds up the steep slope that leads out of the valley. A *voltigeur* officer from the 2/32e Léger encourages his men forward. Two hundred men were organized as the storming party to be followed by another 400; they are *voltigeurs* and *carabiniers* or grenadiers of the 32e Léger, 66e Ligne and 82e Ligne. Their ability to target the riflemen they know are on the slope behind rocks is limited because the dark-coloured British uniforms make seeing them difficult. Their best opportunity will be to close rapidly with the British; however, the rock-strewn slope makes progress beyond the winding path the British are targeting difficult and slow.

Craufurd wanted to conduct a raid on the French siege train at Salamanca, but Wellington vetoed the idea. The French were being delayed enough as they prepared for the siege. On 15 June, the French opened a battery on Ciudad Rodrigo. With the River Águeda now fordable, the Light Division was brought together near Galegos and was on standby to move, but the British made no attempt to attack the besiegers – they could observe what was happening, but did not have the strength to oppose the French. On 27 June, the French crossed the Águeda to the north and south of Ciudad Rodrigo to cut off communication with the garrison entirely. On 10 July the city surrendered.

On 21 July, Ney advanced in force on Craufurd's positions east of the Côa and Craufurd refused to cross the river on 22 or 23 July. The only bridge available to him was 2.5 miles south-west of Almeida. The bridge was hidden from view from the city; Almeida stood on a plateau 200ft above the Côa. The terrain was broken, with numerous enclosures surrounded by stone walls. Ney decided to attack on 24 July to cut off Craufurd. He massed two cavalry brigades in front of 13 battalions of infantry of Loison's 3e Division. Généraux de division Julien Augustin Joseph Mermet and Jean Gabriel Marchand stood behind Loison with their divisions; in total, the French had 16 squadrons and 33 battalions. A heavy storm during the night gave Craufurd the opportunity to withdraw, but he refused to do so that morning before the main attack developed. O'Hare's company was caught by French hussars and lost 56 casualties, but the rest got away when the 1/43rd Light Infantry appeared and gave the French cavalry a volley. Stone walls obstructed the cavalry's pursuit. Craufurd ordered the three British battalions to act as the rearguard for the retreating artillery, baggage, cavalry and Portuguese forces. The road wound down a slope and the infantry got to the approach to the bridge first. A long, sandy hillock covered the crossing point and was held by various companies of the British battalions. Craufurd

Following the surrender of Ciudad Rodrigo on 10 July, Masséna was free to move against the Portuguese fortress town of Almeida. Rather incautiously, Craufurd attempted to shield Almeida by holding a line east of the River Côa with a force of only 3,500 infantry and 1,200 cavalry. On 24 July, the 1/95th retreated from initial positions behind some stone walls to defend a bridge on the Côa in order for other battalions of the Light Division to escape. The men of the 1/95th were nearly cut off by a French attack on a hill above the bridge. Here, the town of Sabugal on the river is shown in an 1812 painting by Thomas Staunton St Clair (1785–1847), who served in the Iberian Peninsula as a junior officer of the 94th Foot and eventually retired as a major-general. (ASKB)

This late-Victorian illustration depicts a riflemen and officer of the 95th in 1814. The 1/95th, serving with the Light Division, retreated into Portugal in the summer of 1810 and would again invade Spain in 1811 after the French attempt to capture Lisbon failed on the defensive lines Wellington had built in front of the city. Along with the 2/95th and the 3/95th, the battalion fought throughout the Peninsular War and was deployed as a battalion at the battle of Tarbes on 20 March 1814 in southern France when an exclusively rifle-armed brigade successfully took a position occupied by French infantry. Britain's riflemen were the best skirmishers the Napoleonic Wars produced. Captain John Blakiston, writing about the battle of Tarbes, would describe them as possessing 'an individual boldness, mutual understanding, and a quickness of eye, in taking advantage of the ground, which, taken altogether, I never saw equalled. They were, in fact, as much superior to the French *voltigeurs*, as the latter were to our skirmishers' (Blakiston 1829: 344). (ASKB)

ordered a withdrawal from the hillock before a portion of the 1/52nd Light Infantry were across the bridge and Beckwith ordered 200 skirmishers from the 1/95th and the 1/43rd Light Infantry to retake the position until they could get across. Elements of Leach's company of the 1/95th then held the bridge to permit some artillery caissons to be harnessed and got away. Craufurd's force had suffered 300 casualties.

Ney wanted to storm across the bridge. Some grenadiers from the 66ᵉ Ligne were repulsed by artillery stationed near the bridge and Portuguese riflemen manning stone walls. Then 300 elite *chasseurs* were ordered to capture the bridge. Four officers and 86 men were killed and three officers and 144 men wounded in the attempt. The 66ᵉ Ligne was ordered in again; the regiment lost its commanding officer and 15 other officers that day. A truce was granted to permit the French to remove their wounded.

The French lost seven officers and 110 men killed, and 17 officers and 393 men wounded; 80 per cent of the casualties were incurred at the bridge. The British lost four officers and 32 men killed and 23 officers and 191 men wounded, with one officer and 82 men missing. In the 1/95th, Captain Creagh died of his wounds, as did Lieutenants Mathias Pratt and Peter Reilly, and five officers were wounded; 12 men were killed and 45 were wounded (some of these died of their wounds); one officer, a sergeant and 52 ranks were taken prisoner. Lieutenant John McCulloch escaped his captors with the assistance of a Spanish family he was billeted with on his march to France. A French hussar grabbed Private Costello of O'Hare's company, but the hussar was shot and Costello got away. He was wounded in the leg before he could cross the bridge, but Private Little bundled him across the bridge although Costello was wounded again by another round (Verner 2015b: 120). Simmons was protected from sabre cuts by his cloak that was strapped across his body and his haversack, but he was hit by a musket ball during the counter-attack on the hillock. The battle had started at 0600hrs and finished at 1600hrs. A rainstorm that lasted throughout the afternoon made keeping powder dry difficult. The brigade withdrew after dark.

Leach detested Craufurd for choosing to fight east of the Côa. One of Wellington's divisional commanders, Major-General Thomas Picton, perhaps out of jealousy of the Light Division's reputation, had refused to offer support to Craufurd. Wellington acknowledged Craufurd's error of judgement. Aware of Picton's role in the affair, he did not censure Craufurd publicly as this would have split the army's officers into rival groupings. In August, the Light Division was divided into two brigades. Beckwith commanded four companies of the 1/95th with the 1/43rd Light Infantry and the 3ª Caçadores. The other four companies accompanied the 1° Caçadores and the 1/52nd Light Infantry. Almeida was invested and soon surrendered when a shell hit the magazine and destroyed most of the guns. On 27 September 1810, while situated on the ridge at Buçaco, the Light Division would encounter Ferey's brigade as they advanced up the slope during the battle and inflict severe casualties upon the French troops. The Anglo-Portuguese withdrawal to Lisbon and the impregnable defensive lines of Torres Vedras would be accomplished successfully.

La Haye Sainte

18 June 1815

BACKGROUND TO BATTLE

Napoleon abdicated on 6 April 1814 and was sent into exile on the island of Elba, but he escaped on 26 February 1815 and returned to Paris on 20 March. He built up his army on the Belgian border. There, the Duke of Wellington (a title bestowed on Wellesley in May 1814) with a multinational army and Blücher with a larger Prussian army were gathering; other allies were preparing to send armies into France. Napoleon needed a rapid victory to prevent an insurmountable coalition force invading France. He decided to move into Belgium and defeat the British and Prussians in detail, prior to other nationalities arriving. He would split his army into two in order to engage both the British and Prussians and have a reserve to be committed to battle against either depending on the tactical merits of the situation. On 15 June 1815 he crossed the border; on 16 June, Ney attacked the British at Quatre Bras and Napoleon with the Imperial Guard was with Maréchal Emmanuel de Grouchy fighting the Prussians at Ligny. Général de division Jean-Baptiste Drouet d'Erlon's 1er Corps was not committed to either battle because of orders from both Napoleon and Ney that had d'Erlon marching and counter-marching between the two encounters. The chance of a decisive French victory at Ligny was lost. Blücher retreated to Wavre and informed Wellington that he would still be able to support him on 18 June.

Napoleon needed to crush Wellington prior to the arrival of the Prussians from the east. Fortifiable buildings were on both flanks of the position Wellington chose and his main position in the centre was situated behind a slope. In the early hours of 18 June, Wellington decided to give battle. On the right (western) flank he sent the Guards Brigade and some Nassauers

The late-war appearance of the *voltigeurs* of the line-infantry regiments is depicted here, along with the company-level *fanion* flag fitted to the musket, here suitably embellished with cornet symbols. (ASKB)

to the complex of buildings at Hougoumont Farm. The villages of La Haye and Papelotte were on the left (eastern) flank; Wellington expected the Prussians to arrive here and had fewer soldiers on that side of the battlefield. Forward of the slope in the centre stood the farm of La Haye Sainte and here Wellington sent elements of the 2nd KGL Brigade from Major-General Charles Alten's 3rd (British) Infantry Division. The brigade's 1st Light Battalion KGL was to the right of the crossroads at the top of the slope; the 8th Line Battalion KGL was to the rear and the 5th Line Battalion KGL was to the right. Just beyond the 1st Light Battalion KGL lay the Lüneburg Light Battalion of the Hanoverian Army. The 2nd Light Battalion KGL was sent to garrison La Haye Sainte. The bulk of the infantry, serving in Lieutenant-General Sir Thomas Picton's 5th (British) Infantry Division, were positioned 440yd back and to the east of the farm.

Alten does not seem to have given the farmhouse top priority. The barn door on the western side of the farm was chopped down to use as firewood on the night of 17/18 June. Major Georg Baring's pioneers were sent to Hougoumont Farm to help build defences there. At La Haye Sainte, loopholes were hewn in the walls of the courtyard. Rifleman Friedrich Lindau was sent to the orchard and had little cover from the incessant rainstorm. He went to the farm and found some wine which he took back to his company. Efforts were in hand to block the barn entrance and build a barricade across the main road flush with the southern end of the farm buildings. Parts of a wagon, farm implements, ladders, chopped-down trees and three spiked French guns were used in the barricade.

After the wet night, the sun was out at 0800hrs the following morning and the rain had stopped. Weapons were cleaned as the men, while seeing the French beginning to manoeuvre on the opposing slopes, prepared for battle. Baring had 377 effectives, including three senior officers and 16 other officers, three surgeons, 24 sergeants, 14 buglers and 317 corporals and riflemen. The surgeons had their casualty clearing station in a hut in the kitchen garden. A company was stationed here and three more were in the orchard. Lieutenants Tobin and Graeme had their companies around the courtyard; the men were placed on the wall, in the farmhouse and on the barricade outside. Two companies of the 1st Light Battalion KGL with Major von dem Busche and two companies of the Hanoverian *Feldjäger* with Major August von Spörken were in skirmish order in front of and to the west of the farm. Two guns were

placed on the main road and two companies of the 1/95th were in a sandpit by the guns, on the eastern side of the road in front of the slope.

Worried that Wellington might elude him, Napoleon sought to punch through Wellington's centre rather than outflank him. Napoleon was not worried about the Prussians because a larger French force was pursuing them. D'Erlon's 1er Corps would move forward east of La Haye Sainte, preceded by a bombardment, in order to capture the farm and then advance to Mont-Saint-Jean to seize the crossroads there. 2e Corps would attack Hougoumont Farm, a move intended to distract Wellington's attention from the centre. D'Erlon decided to use his only light regiment, the 13e Léger, to seize La Haye Sainte. He probably ordered the 2e Division to set off first towards La Haye Sainte even though the division was deployed second in from the main road. Napoleon may have expected the massed French columns to outflank the farm and make the garrison's position untenable. There was no provision to use French artillery against the farm; the buildings were partially hidden in a dip and were a difficult target to hit.

These 1890 illustrations by Charles Lyall (1833–1911) show a rifleman (left) and officer (right) from the 2nd Light Battalion KGL. The battalion had two majors, two captains, nine lieutenants and five ensigns at Waterloo. Of these officers, three would be killed, seven wounded and two taken prisoner. (ASKB)

MAP KEY

1 Night, 17/18 June: Major Georg Baring, with the 2nd Light Battalion KGL, is told to garrison La Haye Sainte. With the barn door on the western side of the farm having been used for firewood, Baring sets his men to building a barricade. Loopholes are hewn in the walls of the courtyard, but with limited success as Baring's pioneers and their entrenching tools have already been sent to Hougoumont Farm.

2 Morning, 18 June: Baring, with three of his companies, is in the orchard to the south of the farm: one company is in the kitchen garden and two are in the courtyard. Two companies of the 1st Light Battalion KGL (Major von dem Busche) and two companies of Hanoverian *Feldjäger* (Major August von Spörken) are in skirmish order in front of the farm.

3 1330hrs, 18 June: Following the French bombardment by the Grande Batterie, Général de division François-Xavier Donzelot's 2e Division advances towards La Haye Sainte. Général de brigade Nicolas Schmitz's brigade (13e Léger and 17e Ligne) moves on the farm from the south and west; Général de brigade Pierre Aulard's brigade moves to the east of the farm.

4 1345hrs, 18 June: Baring and Busche suffer losses and retreat to the barn entrance and ridge. The Lüneburg Light Battalion and two companies of the 1st Light Battalion KGL advance towards La Haye Sainte. The Lüneburg Light Battalion and men from the 1st and 2nd Light battalions KGL are caught by French cavalry and flee up the slope. Most elements of the 2nd Light Battalion KGL soon move back to the farm.

5 1400hrs, 18 June: Aulard's brigade ejects the 1/95th from the sandpit and captures the kitchen garden. The 5th and 8th Line battalions KGL are ordered forward; the 8th Line Battalion KGL is caught in line by French cavalry and is routed.

6 1415hrs, 18 June: The Household and Union Cavalry brigades launch a devastating charge on the French advancing on the slope to the east of La Haye Sainte. French pressure on the farm is relieved.

7 1500–1700hrs, 18 June: Schmitz assaults the barn entrance and the main gate. The attempt to bring down the main gate with axes fails. The barn-entrance barricade holds. The French interrupt their assault to permit the massed French cavalry charge through at 1600hrs. At 1700hrs, Baring sends an officer back to ask for more ammunition. The light-infantry company from the 5th Line Battalion KGL is sent instead.

8 1715–1830hrs, 18 June: A third French assault sets the barn on fire. Having again sent an officer to ask for more ammunition and receiving instead a light company from the 1. Infanterie-Regiment von Nassau and a centre company from the 2. Infanterie-Regiment von Nassau, Baring uses their kettles to put the fire out.

9 1900hrs, 18 June: The French mount a final assault, conducted by the 13e Léger with Général de brigade Jean-Gaudens-Claude Pegot's brigade (4e Division) in support; the attackers succeed in breaking down the main gate and barn-entrance barricade. Baring's riflemen have no ammunition and he orders a retreat through the kitchen garden. The French from the farm fire on the ridge and bring up horse artillery. The 2nd Light Battalion KGL slowly starts to lose cohesion. Baring is wounded, but his despair is fleeting as the general advance is soon sounded to pursue the retreating French off the battlefield.

Battlefield environment

La Haye Sainte was a walled farmhouse compound at the foot of an escarpment on the Charleroi–Brussels road that dominated the centre of Wellington's line at Waterloo. On the southern side there was an orchard and in the rear a kitchen garden, bounded by a small wall towards the road and by a hedge on the other sides. Two doors and three large gates led from the courtyard to the exterior. The walled area was composed of a farmhouse, stables and piggery. During the night of 17/18 June, the barn door to the courtyard of the farm was used as firewood. The door that led from the courtyard to the exterior through the archway was still blocking entry that way. A smaller door near the farmhouse led out to the main road; another led from the pond to the orchard.

The 2nd Light Battalion KGL had to fortify La Haye Sainte in haste. Baring placed three companies in the orchard: one was in the kitchen garden and two were in the courtyard. He recalled how he was instructed to send his battalion pioneers to Hougoumont Farm (quoted in Lindau 2009: 186). The mule with the entrenching tools had been lost the previous day. Loopholes were hewn in the walls of the courtyard, but the barn entrance was not blocked effectively. Here, Rifleman Lindau would receive a head wound; he refused treatment in order to stay at his position and would receive the Guelphic Medal for his bravery. The riflemen in La Haye Sainte would not have enough rifle ammunition and could not use musket balls, as they were too large for the Baker rifle. The cart that carried the brigade's ammunition had broken down. Even if this had not happened, the barn and farmyard gate that provided access to the farm from the main road were situated on the dangerous eastern side, exposed to French fire.

Joseph Gastinieau

Joseph Gastinieau was born in 1789 and conscripted into the 13e Léger in May 1808. He was on garrison duty with the depot and was promoted to *caporal* in April 1809 and *sergent-major* in 1811. He took recruits from the depot to the field battalions in time for Napoleon's invasion of Russia in June 1812. He fought at the battles of Smolensk on 16–18 August and Borodino on 7 September. He was captured during the retreat and for two years was a prisoner-of-war. He was released in 1814 and marched 500 miles to France later that year. He was the *adjudant-chef* of the 13e Léger during the Waterloo campaign of June–July 1815. He was with the 13e Léger during the attack on La Haye Sainte on 17–18 June and would have kept close to Colonel Gougeon.

After 1815, Gastinieau served in the French Army in the Mayenne Legion, in 1818 with the rank of *lieutenant* and then *capitaine*. In 1823, he participated in the campaign to restore King Ferdinand VII to the Spanish throne. In 1840 he was promoted *major* and posted to the 23e Léger; he also served in the 46e Ligne during 1841–45. He was awarded the Royal Order of the Légion d'honneur. He retired in 1845 and died in 1873.

French troops surrendered to the KGL personnel; the cavalry led them back to allied lines.

Baring was then able to return to the farm and the 1/95th was back in the sandpit. Baring had three officers dead and six wounded, and 70 other ranks dead, seriously wounded or taken prisoner; 300 of his battalion remained, augmented by some Lüneburgers and men from Busche's battalion. He asked for reinforcements and was sent two companies of the 1st Light Battalion KGL, commanded by Captain Henry von Marschalck and Captain von Gilsa, which Baring placed in the kitchen garden. On the French side, Aulard, the brigade commander, and Colonel Jean Antoine Rignon, the commanding officer of the 51e Ligne, were dead or mortally wounded, as were two battalion commanders.

The stout buildings of La Haye Sainte could not be brought down with the field artillery available to the French. Bringing up French guns to fire at the main gate would be risky because the crews could be targeted. Schmitz was still near the orchard. The farm was serving to break the cohesion of the French advance on Wellington's centre. At 1500hrs, Ney ordered two columns to attack La Haye Sainte, supported by two sapper companies. At the barricade, Graeme and Lindau could see French columns approaching with skirmishers in the lead. The skirmishers were driven back, however, and the KGL withdrew to the main gate once the columns were close. Graeme ordered Lindau to bar the main gate. From loopholes near the gateway, the KGL troops fired into the dense mass of French infantry outside; having shot, a rifleman stepped back to reload and make room for those who were ready to fire. At times, the French would gain a loophole and fire through the aperture, causing casualties. Some KGL personnel on top of the piggery were also hit. Five KGL soldiers, including Corporal Riemstedt and Riflemen Lindenau and Lindhorst, drove the French from the loopholes while French troops armed with axes attempted to hack down the main gate. At the same time, the barn entrance was attacked. Rifleman Ludwig Dahrendorf stayed at his post here despite three bayonet wounds. Rifleman Friedrich Hegener suffered a bayonet wound in the leg and refused to have the surgeon attend to it. In the courtyard, Baring had his horse shot from under him.

At 1500hrs, when this second assault had started, the 5th Line Battalion KGL was ordered forward to the farm. The battalion had to form square

and was still in this formation when the massed French cavalry charges on the British centre began at 1600hrs. The French infantry attacks on La Haye Sainte slackened as they made way for their cavalry to pass. Some of Baring's men went through the barn entrance to fire at the cavalry as they charged between La Haye Sainte and Hougoumont Farm. When the cavalry were initially repulsed, the French infantry temporarily retired with them.

Lindau targeted a mounted enemy officer he had noticed leading the French forward. The mount toppled on top of the officer when hit. Lindau was part of a sally that went forth from the gateway to drive the French back. He reached the officer and used his rifle butt to hit him on the head. Lindau plundered him and, when enemy cavalry approached, made his way back to the barricade. In the farm Lindau asked Baring to look after a bag of gold coins he had taken from another Frenchman, but Baring refused.

The fighting only diminished at 1700hrs. At this point, Baring dispatched an officer to ask for more ammunition. There was plenty with the 1/95th in the sandpit, but Baring did not ask them. No cart could successfully negotiate the area from the ridge to the farm because French skirmishers were interdicting this approach. Cartridges and ball ammunition would soon be in demand.

At 1700hrs, Napoleon ordered a brigade from Général de division Pierre François Joseph Durutte's 4e Division on the right to reinforce the French attack near the farm. Prior to the arrival of this brigade, the French started a third assault on the farm. Smoke from the burning barn concealed the approach of two French columns. Lindau was ordered to the main gate when the French approached. When a rifleman fell, Lindau immediately went through his pockets to search for cartridges. Baring rode around to reassure his soldiers that ammunition was on the way. Lindau was hit in the head and was ordered by Lieutenant Ole Lindam to seek medical attention. Lindau refused; instead, he poured rum on his scarf, got a rifleman to tie the scarf around his head, and tied his shako to his pack. Lindam rebuked him and told him not to present so much of a target, at which point Lindam was hit in the hand. Lindau told him to go back but Lindam also refused.

At 1700hrs, Wellington ordered forward the 5th Line Battalion KGL. On two occasions after the battalion received the order, the KGL troops managed to form square just in time to stop a French cavalry charge. Captain Christian von Wurmb's light company, armed with muskets, was detached from the battalion to reinforce Baring. Wurmb was hit by artillery and killed before he got there, as were 14 others; 85 entered the farm. Musket-armed Nassauers from the Flanquer-Compagnie of the II. Bataillon, 1. Infanterie-Regiment von Nassau were also sent; again, the company commander, Captain Karl Joseph von Weitershausen, was killed before reaching the farm. A centre company from the I. Bataillon, 2. Infanterie-Regiment von Nassau that was garrisoning Hougoumont Farm probably also reinforced Baring.

Instead of forcing the entrance to the barn, the French in their third assault set the barn on fire. Lindau heard a cry from the barn entrance. He dashed to the barn and could see smoke. Baring and Sergeant Reese were taking kettles the Nassauers had brought with them, filling them up in a pond and trying to put the fire out. Near the pond, Riemstedt, Lindenau and Lindhorst were using their swords to hack at the arms of French soldiers pointing their muskets through the loopholes. Between 1800hrs and 1830hrs, the French retreated again.

The 13e Léger, fighting alongside the brigade from Durutte's 4e Division advancing up the ridge, soon started the fourth attack. The barn entrance was assailed at the same time as the main gate. Again, the barn was set on fire; again, the fire was put out. Baring sent another plea for ammunition, stating that he would have to leave the position if nothing was sent. The loopholes in the courtyard were weakly manned and the French were maintaining heavy fire through some. Lindau thought he noticed French fire lessening and went back to the loopholes. As he put his rifle through a loophole and fired, a Frenchman seized the barrel. Lindau called out to another rifleman what had happened and the soldier fired through the loophole, forcing the Frenchman to release Baring's weapon. Then the rifle was grabbed again; this time a KGL bayonet was thrust through and Lindau managed to withdraw his rifle. While he was reloading, the French fired a hail of bullets. Lindau's rifle was hit and broken. He soon found a replacement and took his place at the loophole once again. Searching through the pockets of fallen men was failing to yield cartridges or ball ammunition, however. The pressure from the French steadily increased. Baring told Lindau to retire, but he refused. He was forced into the courtyard when the French climbed on top of the walls and had broken through the main gate with axes. Then the French climbed onto the piggery. With no ammunition remaining, Lindau bayoneted a French soldier; the sword-bayonet was bent as a result of Lindau's action and could not be used again. The French were also pressing in through the barn entrance. In the face of these developments, Baring gave the order to retire into the kitchen garden. Fearing the bad impression this would have on the men, he sent three officers

The struggle for La Haye Sainte

The French have attacked the farm of La Haye Sainte since early afternoon. By the early evening, *voltigeurs* and *chasseurs* from the 13e Léger, having burst through the main-gate entrance, have entered the courtyard. With his men out of ammunition, Major Baring, the commander of the 2nd Light Battalion KGL, has ordered a retreat through the farmhouse to the kitchen garden. He has asked Lieutenant Graeme to stay at the entrance to the farmhouse until all those that could escape have done so; their only route is along the narrow passageway that leads to the north side of the farm. The riflemen use their sword-bayonets to defend themselves as they are out of ammunition. Musket-armed personnel of the light company of the 5th Line Battalion KGL, sent in the late afternoon to reinforce the garrison, are still able to fire their weapons. Soon the French will seize Graeme; he will struggle free, however, and evade the bullets fired by his pursuers into the passageway.

to the farmhouse to stay there until all the men had left. At the entrance to the farmhouse, Lindau noticed Lindum fighting hand to hand.

Baring went to the kitchen garden and ordered the company there, now commanded by Corporal Henry Müller, to head towards the main allied position. A French soldier was about to shoot Ensign George Frank and Graeme stabbed him with his sword. Then, near the farmhouse, Frank stabbed a Frenchman who was levelling his musket at Graeme. An irate French officer grabbed Graeme by the collar and some soldiers were going to bayonet the British officer, but he parried with his sword. The French looked frightened and pale. Graeme broke free and bolted off along the corridor through the farmhouse, two shots missing him as he went. The French stormed into the farmhouse. The passageways inside were narrow. Frank pierced a pursuer with his sabre, but then his arm was broken by a French musket ball. He sought refuge in a bedroom, hid behind a bed, and when two riflemen also entered the room witnessed them being shot by two Frenchmen following them. Frank remained undiscovered and revealed himself only when the British retook the farm.

Lindau found himself surrounded by Frenchmen in the courtyard. He struck out with the butt of his rifle and managed to break free. Then a soldier grabbed his clothes while another was about to bayonet him; Lindau pivoted and the soldier was bayoneted instead. He decided to enter the barn and escape that way having seen Captain Ernest Holtzermann taken there by the French; when Lindau reached the barn, however, he found too many of the enemy and was also taken prisoner. The prisoners were brought to the main gate and onto the main road where they were robbed. Lindau lost his bag of gold coins and Holtzermann's sash and scabbard were torn from him. The prisoners were furious, but Holtzermann calmed the situation. Cavalry escorted them back to French lines. Lindau escaped during the night and managed to get a drink from a German serving in the French ranks.

With the farmhouse captured by the French, keeping hold of the kitchen garden was not an option for the defenders. The French brought horse artillery to within 330yd of the British line; infantry could fire from the farmhouse and kitchen garden against the main British line, too. French cavalry re-appeared. Ney had wanted to bring up the Imperial Guard, but Napoleon had refused. Despite this, losses to the KGL units and nearby British battalions were increasing. Baring sent back the men from battalions other than his own, and then attached his KGL soldiers to two companies from the 1st Light Battalion KGL, situated alongside the road by the hollow north of the farm. They were fired upon from the farm; Marschalck was killed and Gilsa had his right arm shattered, as did Graeme. At 1930hrs, the 5th Line Battalion KGL was ordered to retake the farm; deploying from square to line, it headed off towards the kitchen garden. The presence of French cavalry should have deterred the KGL line infantrymen. They were soon set upon by cavalry who inflicted terrible losses; the cavalry were only stopped by a volley at 20yd from the KGL light infantryman in the road by the hollow before British hussars drove them off.

Then Baring had a horse shot from under him that pinned him to the ground. He was freed, though his leg was injured. Separated from what was left of his battalion, Baring sought refuge in a nearby building; by the time he procured another horse to return to the hollow, his men were nowhere to be seen. Some had gone to search for ammunition in the rear; his battalion had started to disintegrate. By then the battle was won, the Imperial Guard thrown in late between Hougoumont Farm and La Haye Sainte having been repulsed and the Prussians having arrived in large numbers. The 2nd Light Battalion KGL had only 42 men in the ranks that were fit and ready to fight. The battalion had lost 34 killed, including three officers, and 112

This illustration depicts a light-infantry officer of one of the KGL's line-infantry battalions in the uniform worn after 1812. Note the corded sash, green light-company plume and distinctive gold officer's 'wings' on the shoulders. (ASKB)

were wounded, including seven officers. Many of the wounded would not recover. French casualties around La Haye Sainte were in the region of 2,000.

Baring's battalion had shown a high degree of cohesion that stemmed from an inherent trust and respect that existed between officers and men. The rank and file wanted to be held in high regard by their officers. They knew that their officers would not risk their lives needlessly. They would fight as long as they had ammunition. When Baring realized that his men had no cartridges and that resistance was futile, he ordered the retreat. The bond between pairs of riflemen that supported each other also improved the cohesion of the battalion. They did not fight because they feared discipline; rather, they fought for ideas of German nationalism. The garrison of La Haye Sainte was from disparate battalions, not just from Hanover. What they did have in common was that they were German.

Analysis

At Roliça, riflemen proved their effectiveness in the assault on an enemy position that had plenty of brush and cover in which to hide during the approach up steep slopes. Whereas the line infantrymen were more naturally inclined to move up the gullies, the riflemen in open formation were capable of operating on the slopes and still making progress. When the line infantry did use the gullies, a counter-attack mounted by the French line battalions drove them back. Instead of using a close-order formation that made a vulnerable target, Fane's Brigade was less vulnerable in dispersed formation and could more effectively target the enemy. The capable skirmishers of the 3/2e Léger could only hinder their momentum rather than stop them. Wellesley always had a sufficient numerical superiority to make a flanking move by Ferguson count, and the main attack if delayed would have moved against a French force that probably would have already started to retreat.

The 3/2e Léger fought an effective delaying action on the hill by Roliça that gained the time Delaborde needed to move his other battalions back to the main position on the ridge at Zambujeira. Here they were heavily outnumbered by the riflemen and though they did have the high ground and could take cover in scrub, their adversaries could similarly benefit from cover in their approach to the hill and could present a harder target, hiding behind rocks as they skirmished forward. The limited range of the muskets compared to the rifles would have permitted the riflemen to stand off out of range and snipe at their targets. The riflemen were not pressed in terms of time, waiting as they were for the enveloping force to appear; they probably pushed on further than they needed to, however, as casualties were not light and were probably inflicted in the main by the 3/2e Léger, and skirmishers from other battalions. The 3/4e Léger could perhaps have added to the skirmisher screen, but they might have deployed on the other flank; the sources are unclear. The attack on the 29th Foot was led by the 70e Ligne; that regiment's two

companies of *voltigeurs* might have helped, although the detachment of three companies to Bombarral to cover Ferguson's approach might have included the *voltigeurs*. Also unclear is whether the rearguard that covered Delaborde's retreat was provided by the 3/2ᵉ Léger or the 3/4ᵉ Léger. The retreat was a hasty affair, with three guns being taken by the British. With Ferguson closing in on the narrow pass from the east, the French infantry would have been keen to get a move on. Instead, the French cavalry was relied upon to discourage the British pursuit.

In the action at Barba del Puerco, the slower rate of fire of riflemen was not such an issue because the enemy could not fire effectively as they did not have any indication where the British were until the riflemen fired. Even then, the French only could notice a spark of gunpowder. The French moved rapidly up the slope to close with the British to limit the number of rounds that the riflemen could fire. The steepness and the rocky nature of the slope disadvantaged the French, however; the moonlight shining on the white cross-belts of the French exposed them to the rifle fire, and the sudden appearance of Major-General Sir Thomas Beckwith with two companies discouraged them further. Craufurd wrote that the battle was the type that riflemen of other nations would shun because the rifle was thought to be less than ideal in close action with an enemy armed with the musket and bayonet. Barba del Puerco proved to Craufurd that the rifle was a weapon that a British soldier could use to defeat the French in the closest fight and regardless of the manner in which the French were armed (Cusick 2013: 129).

For his part, Ferey followed best practice by assembling a composite force of *voltigeurs* and grenadiers to attack the bridge. The *voltigeurs* of the 32ᵉ Léger

This illustration depicts a rifleman of the 95th firing his rifle in 1808. On campaign, the Light Division provided the advance guard and rearguard and manned the outposts of Wellington's army. On the battlefield, they protected the line against enemy skirmishers and in the advance harassed and unsettled the enemy line, sniping at officers and gun crew, wearing down the physical and psychological strength of the enemy. The rifle-armed troops at Wellington's disposal, including the 95th, the 5/60th and the two light-infantry battalions of the KGL, were the best skirmishers of the Napoleonic Wars. The combat encounters in the Iberian Peninsula showed the increasing importance placed upon riflemen in the British Army. Mostly they were supported by musket-armed troops, but by 1814 the riflemen could defeat musket-armed troops on their own. (ASKB) were probably leading the attack; those of the 66e and 82e Ligne were probably following on. The 32e Léger personnel were aided by the loud noise created by the river and effectively surprised the sentinels, although not without a warning shot being fired. The French needed to reach the ridgeline prior to Beckwith's arrival. The slope was steep enough in places to restrict the French to a limited number of routes, however, and the riflemen knew to target these paths as they had garrisoned the area for long enough to be familiar with the terrain. The French had also conducted sorties that had taken them across the bridge in the preceding days, but the soldiers who had taken part in the sorties were probably not those engaged in this attack. Ferey's brigade had only recently deployed to the area; his men had not spent time on reconnaissance. Within 330yd of the bridge the slope climbed more than 100m in elevation. The path wound back and forth; following this would have made the French vulnerable indeed to the rifles' fire. This is what they had to do to make the ridge in time.

The importance of riflemen in defending buildings or fortifications could be debated when looking at the role played by the 2nd Light Battalion KGL at La Haye Sainte in June 1815. The riflemen's slow rate of fire and the reliance on what was a more limited supply of specialist ammunition were detrimental factors. Light infantry possessing the same tactical skill-sets in operating in dispersed groups, armed with muskets that could fire more rapidly, might have held out for longer. A light-infantry battalion or composite battalion of light-infantry companies reinforced by a rifle company or two would probably have lasted longer; however, by 1815 the KGL battalions were exclusively armed with rifles, and sending musket-armed companies as reinforcements to make up for the lack of rifle ammunition was a case of too little, too late. The importance of the farm was not thoroughly appreciated; if it had been, the KGL troops would have retained the barn door and retained their pioneer tools to knock through more loopholes and build a firing platform around the wall. The potential shortage of ammunition needed to be established, and supplies from the 1/95th utilized.

The French did not fully appreciate the importance of La Haye Sainte either. Rather than committing an entire division to capture the farm in the initial assault, only a single brigade was sent, first going to the orchard and then to the west of the farm. The other brigade seems to have bypassed the farm during the advance to the ridge and the sandpit. The 13e Léger was the most appropriate French unit to send against the farm and Donzelot's 2e Division, although formed up second in from the left, with the regiment serving as part of Schmitz's brigade, moved ahead of the 1er Division. The 13e Léger near the orchard could withstand the British cavalry charge that threw d'Erlon's men back from the ridge. The regiment's persistence in organizing multiple attacks during the day finally paid off. By that point, however, Napoleon did not have enough time to beat Wellington prior to the full-scale arrival of the Prussians, and his reluctance to commit the Imperial Guard gave Wellington time to re-organize his defences. If the Imperial Guard had advanced close behind the massed cavalry during mid-afternoon, even if La Haye Sainte had not been taken, the Guardsmen might have broken the British squares behind the ridge. The allied forces in La Haye Sainte, attacked by the 13e Léger, would not have had the opportunity to fire on the Imperial Guard.

This *voltigeur* of the 88ᵉ Ligne wears a version of the summer campaign dress worn in the Iberian Peninsula, eschewing his *habit* in favour of the sleeved waistcoat and wearing baggy trousers made from local cloth. As with all French canteens of the era, this man's is a privately obtained example; there was no official issue, unlike in the British Army. (ASKB)

88ᵉ de Ligne.
Voltigeur.

Pierre Albert
Leroux

Aftermath

The 5/60th fought throughout the Peninsular War and won a distinguished reputation, gaining 16 battle honours. In 1816 the 5/60th was disbanded along with the partly rifle-armed 7/60th, which had served in the War of 1812 in North America; the rifle heritage of the regiment was perpetuated, though, in the redesignation of the regiment first as the 60th (The Duke of York's Own Rifle Corps) Regiment of Foot in 1824 and then as the 60th (The King's Royal Rifle Corps) Regiment of Foot on the accession of William IV to the British throne in June 1830. The regiment served in numerous Victorian conflicts and both World Wars; today, its heritage is perpetuated in the British Army's 2nd Battalion, The Rifles. Its matchless combat reputation bolstered by the many veterans in its ranks who wrote well-received memoirs, the 95th was spared the post-war cuts in recognition of its crucial battlefield role and was redesignated The Rifle Brigade in February 1816, with the Duke of Wellington as its Colonel-in-Chief from 1820 until his death in 1852. As with the 60th, the unit gave distinguished service over two centuries and remains in the present-day British Army's order of battle as 4th Battalion, The Rifles.

The 2ᵉ Léger served in the Iberian Peninsula until 1813, when it joined Napoleon's forces fighting in Germany and saw action during the invasion of France in 1814. It took the field again in 1815 and fought at Ligny and Waterloo. The 13ᵉ Léger never served in the Iberian Peninsula, but won battle honours at Austerlitz (1805), Jena (1806), Eylau (1807), Eckmühl and Wagram (both 1809) before fighting in Russia and Germany in 1812–13, and then at Waterloo (1815). After service in the Iberian Peninsula, the 32e Léger fought in Germany in 1813; it was disbanded after April 1814 and did not take the field in 1815. All of the French light-infantry regiments were broken up after Napoleon's second exile to St Helena, with individual battalions joining the departmental legions that replaced the regiments of France's armed forces; the light-infantry traditions of the French Army survived and

thrived, though, and terms such as *voltigeur* and *chasseur* have continued to be used in the subsequent two centuries of warfare.

A 19th-century German depiction of the 1st Light Battalion KGL. The KGL was disbanded in 1816; from their pensions, the officers of the 2nd Light Battalion KGL set up a fund for the widows and orphans of fallen KGL soldiers. Georg Baring was given a baronetcy and retired from the army of the Kingdom of Hanover as a *Generalleutnant*; Ernest Holtzermann retired as a *Generalmajor*. Rifleman Friedrich Lindau recovered from his wounds in Brussels and was discharged in October 1815. (The Print Collector/Print Collector/Getty Images)

Dating from 1828, this French illustration shows a Napoleonic-era French skirmisher taking ammunition from the cartridge pouch of a fallen comrade. (Art Media/ Print Collector/Getty Images)

UNIT ORGANIZATIONS

British

In theory, a rifle battalion had ten companies, each with eight 12-man sections; this is how the 5/60th was organized in 1808. Captains commanded companies, each assisted by an ensign and two lieutenants. In reality, most companies had only four sections organized into two platoons, as was the case with the 1/95th at Barba del Puerco. A lieutenant would command each platoon; ideally, a sergeant, assisted by a corporal, led each section. Sometimes the captain would not be present, and a lieutenant would command the company. While after 1808 the 5/60th would more often than not deploy individual companies to support every British brigade operating in the Iberian Peninsula, the 1/95th and the 2nd Light Battalion KGL operated as complete battalions.

French

In 1808, a light-infantry regiment typically included four *bataillons de guerre* (some had seven), each with six companies (one *carabinier*, one *voltigeur* and four *chasseur* companies). A *chef de bataillon* commanded each battalion, aided by his adjutant and the adjutant's assistant. A *capitaine* commanded the company; a *lieutenant* and *sous-lieutenant* assisted him. In theory, the company establishment included a *sergent-major*, four *sergents*, a *caporal-fourrier*, eight *caporaux*, two drummers or cornetists and 121 privates.

BIBLIOGRAPHY

Arvers, Capitaine P. (1876). *Historique du 82ᵉ Régiment d'Infanterie de Ligne*. Paris: Typographie Lahure.

Barbero, A. (2005). *The Battle. A New History of Waterloo*. London: Atlantic Publishing.

Beamish, Maj. N.L. (1832–37). *History of the King's German Legion*, vols 1 and 2. London: T. & W. Boone.

Blakiston, J. (1829). *Twelve Years Military Adventure in Three Quarters of The Globe, Vol. 2*. London: Colborn.

Butler, Lt-Col. L. (1913). *The Annals of the King's Royal Rifles Corps*, vol. 1. London: Smith, Elder & Co.

Butler, Lt-Col. Lewis (1923). *The Annals of the King's Royal Rifle Corps*, vol. 2. London: John Murray.

Chappell, M. (2000a). *The King's German Legion (1): 1803–12*. Men-at-Arms 338. Oxford: Osprey.

Chappell, M. (2000b). *The King's German Legion (1): 1812–16*. Men-at-Arms 339. Oxford: Osprey.

Coppens, B. (with P. Courcelle) (2000). *La Haie-Sainte, Waterloo 1815*. Les Carnets de la Campagne 3 Brussels: Tondeur Diffusion.

Crowdy, T. (2002). *French Napoleonic Infantryman*. Warrior 57. Oxford: Osprey.

Crowdy, T. (2012). *Incomparable: Napoleon's 9th Light Infantry Regiment*. Oxford: Osprey.

Cusick, R. (2013). *Wellington's Rifles: The Origins, Development and Battles of the Rifle Regiments in the Peninsular War and at Waterloo from 1758–1815*. Barnsley: Pen & Sword.

Fosten, B. (1982). *Wellington's Infantry (2)*. Men-at-Arms 119. Oxford: Osprey.

Griffith, R. (2019). *Riflemen: The History of the 5th Battalion, 60th (Royal American) Regiment 1797–1818*. Warwick: Helion.

Haythornthwaite, P. (2002). *British Rifleman 1797–1815*. Warrior 47. Oxford: Osprey.

Lindau, F., ed. J. Bogle & A. Uffindell (2009). *A Waterloo Hero. The Reminiscences of Friedrich Lindau*. London: Frontline Books.

Muir, R. (1998). *Tactics and the Experiences of Battle in the Age of Napoleon*. New Haven, CT: Yale University Press.

Ross-Lewin, H. (1904). *With the 32nd in the Peninsula*. Dublin: Hodges.

Sherer, M. (1827). *Recollections of the Peninsula*. London: Longman, Rees, Orme & Green.

Simmons, G. (1899). *A British Rifleman*. London: A & C. Black.

Simms, B. (2014). *The Longest Afternoon: The 400 Men who Decided the Battle of Waterloo*. London: Penguin.

Urban, M. (2003). *Rifles: Six Years with Wellington's Legendary Sharpshooters*. London: Faber & Faber.

Verner, W. (2015a). *History and Campaigns of the Rifle Brigade, 1800–1809*. Pickle Partners Publishing.

Verner, W. (2015b). *History and Campaigns of the Rifle Brigade, 1809–1814*. Pickle Partners Publishing.

These re-enactors depicting riflemen of the 1/95th have fixed sword-bayonets to their rifles. The sword-bayonet had a 23in-long blade that was intended for personal protection and was also employed to help make camp and cut firewood. The Baker rifle could not be fired with the sword-bayonet fixed as this made the weapon too muzzle-heavy and holding the aim was not achievable. All three battalions of the 95th fought at Waterloo on 18 June 1815, but the 2/95th and 3/95th were not deployed as skirmishers and fought in line. Three companies of the 1/95th were in the sandpit near La Haye Sainte and three others were the supports on the ridge behind. Leach, Simmons and Fairfoot all survived the battle; the 1/95th's dispersed formation would mean that the battalion's casualties were relatively low, with many of the wounded sustaining only light wounds. (Stephen Bardens/Getty Images)

INDEX